Waking Up Cattywampus

Memoir of a Transplanted Southerner

Steven Powers Chylinski

Copyright © 2019 Steven Powers Chylinski

All rights reserved.

This book or any portion thereof may not be reproduced or used without the express written permission of the author.

Dedication

This memoir is dedicated to the memories of
Steve J. Chylinski and Ruby Mae Powers Chylinski
whose contributions made this
life of mine possible.

Contents

Prologue	1
Foreword	4
Overview	6

ACT ONE: CHILDHOOD

Scene 1	Eating dirty orange peels	11
Scene 2	There goes the ankle	16
Scene 3	Mom and dad tell me who I am	18
Scene 4	The bashful kid and the spelling bee	22
Scene 5	Graduating Harvard, going to Mars	24
Scene 6	Dogs, babies, birds, Buddy & Brian	27
Scene 7	Mamaw & me down by the White Castle®	31
Scene 6	Mama, me, and alcoholism	35
Scene 10	Pica and a security blanket	38

ACT TWO: ADOLESCENCE

Scene 1	Poverty, hunger, and the "Butcher"	43
Scene 2	Gun battle in the gully	46
Scene 3	Loneliness and the "goody-two-shoes"	49

| Scene 4 | The nun suggests a future | 52 |
| Scene 5 | Objects of affection: Rudy Regalado and Ann Rudniski | 54 |

ACT THREE: EARLY ADULTHOOD

Scene 1	Mackerel-snappers make the best marines	59
Scene 2	Sink or swim: Stormy times ahead	63
Scene 3	Meeting K. at the Quarries	69
Scene 4	Marriage & the domestic Peace Corps	73
Scene 5	Love letters: Songs from the heart	79
Scene 6	I could teach what and where	81

ACT FOUR: MIDDLE AGE

Scene 1	Karla asks for a divorce	85
Scene 2	Angst and profligate behavior	88
Scene 3	A remarriage: Pain that may never end	91
Scene 4	Meeting Sheila	94
Scene 5	Not Catholic enough	99
Scene 6	Down under, South American-style	105

ACT FIVE: OLD AGE

Scene 1	Illness and beliefs: Chlotilde & Clovis	115
Scene 2	The inevitable end	119
Scene 3	Telling tales out of school	123
Scene 4	Milestones	127

Scene 5	The future not yet written	129

Reflecting on my search for identity	133
References	168
Appendices:	
1. The path from William Henry Powers to Clovis I	172
2. Mary Underwood's ancestors in America	175
3. Some male ancestors allied with the Powers' family	176
4. Ancestors of William Henry Powers who bore his name	178
5. A letter written to my younger self	179
6. A history of story-telling	181
7. Fifty-two American Southernisms	183
Also by the author	185

Prologue

It was a cold and dreary Saturday morning in February 2011 in a fashionable Cleveland, Ohio suburb. Earlier that day, I had received a telephone call from the caregivers at the assisted living site where my ailing and aged parents lived. It was a comfortable setting that from the exterior appeared to be just another private home on a suburban, upper-middle-class street. The building was indistinguishable from the other dwellings on that thoroughfare.

The call from the nurse who owned the facility was one that I had probably dreaded since childhood. The voice on the other end of the line began, "I am afraid I have some bad news for you." Filled as I was with a sense of foreboding, I suspected what was coming next.

"Your father is not doing well," the nurse announced. Was this health care code for "Your dad is dying?" It was. With trepidation, I responded shakily, "Wha', Wha', What's wrong?" For a minute, all stopped including my breathing. I am sure that Mrs. Watson (not her real name) was as delicate as she knew how, but there is no easy way to say to a family member, "Your father may be nearing the end." She added, "You will want to come here as soon as possible."

And she was right about Dad's demise. Still, I thought to myself, "Modern medicine could surely save him. For God's sake, a world-renowned hospital in Cleveland was now performing *face transplants*." Surely, it could buy my childhood hero a few extra months or even years.

My father died like he had lived—in a grandiose manner that belied his 5 feet, 6 inch stature. As he lay dying, the 25 by 30 foot living space that he shared with my mother was quite large, and contained relatively little furniture—a bed, two dressers, and a small, well-worn night stand. The shades and drapes were tightly drawn shut even though it was 10:00 a.m. The dim light gave the room an air of a 19th century Charles Dickens novel. The scene where Ebenezer Scrooge was awakened by the Ghost of Christmas Past comes to mind here. The room's temperature seemed quite high and it felt stuffy, like the air decided to stop moving in deference to the unfolding events.

There was plenty of room for visitors in the spacious area allotted to my parents. Like some papal audience, my father's space was filled with perhaps as many as two dozen nieces, nephews, grandchildren, adult children, and assorted friends and acquaintances—all keeping vigil over a 93-year-old, bed-ridden man who passed alternately into and out of consciousness. I spent much of that Saturday quietly grieving, although Dad was still officially alive. A former teacher of mine, Elizabeth Kubler-Ross, has called this kind of grief *anticipatory*. The term fits well.

Butterflies fluttering around in my stomach, I thought to myself in a panic, "Oh, my God. Is this it? Is my father going to leave me alone, putting me on the road to adult orphan-hood? Will my sense of who I am (e.g. a son) need to shift again?"

I had spent the first several decades of my life trying to discover who I really was at my core. Of course, life has a way of throwing curves at us when instead we were expecting a fastball straight down the middle. A marriage, the birth of children, a move to the Caribbean, a divorce, a string of college degrees, and a series of prestigious jobs had all forced me to somewhat alter who I thought I was. And now my parents' illnesses and inevitable deaths would force me to reassess my identity once again. If my parents died, mine would be the next generation to pass away. Somehow, I would now be officially old.

I ignored the weather outside, my own hunger pangs and the tears in my eyes and in mother's. I felt helpless. I was in no way prepared to willingly let my father go. Yet, what could I do but sit quietly while I experienced my own fear and pain, awaiting the end. It was a time I would never forget.

Suddenly, I remembered a friend telling me, perhaps as much as thirty years earlier, about his final hours with his own father who lay ill in a bed in South Dakota. Could I muster the same kind of courage that Andrew had shown in the 1980s? I made up my mind to give that behavior a try.

We were not a touchy-feely family, and I can recall almost no soft, tender, physical moments with my father. Once, after attending an emotion-packed workshop designed to get counselors in touch with their feelings, wants and needs, I had cornered my father in his bedroom on Twin Oaks Drive. I swallowed my fears, and I begged my father "Do you love me, Dad?" He blustered, hemmed, and hawed, but in the end, he said simply, "Yes, I love you, son"

And again, in the late 1990s when my younger brother died under mysterious and suspicious circumstances, my father sidled up to me at Richard's wake, and said almost in a whisper, "A father should never have to bury his son." As he said these words, he gently laid his head on my shoulder for what seemed like minutes. I muttered a reply that sounded something like, "No, it seems so unfair!" or other innocuous words. This was an unforgettable moment of support and tenderness that I will cherish.

Yet, if this was to be the end for him and for our relationship, then maybe, just maybe, I should take one final opportunity to express the depth of my love for this man. I took a deep breath, and committed myself to take what seemed like a big risk with my father. "Ready or not Dad, here I come."

But, I am getting ahead of my story here. Let's hope that Shakespeare (1606) was wrong when he said in *Macbeth*, "Life's but a walking shadow, a poor player, that struts and frets his hour upon the stage and then is heard no more; it is a tale told by an idiot, full of sound and fury, signifying nothing (Act V, Scene V)."

Shakespeare was right about one thing and that is, a life as it transpires is like a play. It contains a series of acts, scenes, and perhaps an intermission or two (and with some refreshments including that old standby, popcorn). Every life has a plot complete with twists and turns, characters, a beginning and an end.

Still, each life has meaning, at least for the one who lives that life. From my early childhood on, I seem to have been concerned about what I stood for, what I wanted to do with my time here on earth. I craved a firm, and preferably succinct, answer to the question, "Who am I?" Perhaps by reflecting on my life, I can now answer this pressing question for myself. We shall see!

Foreword

A writer friend once told me that she always knows a writer when she meets one by how much they talk. Writers like to talk, she says, and when there's nobody around to listen, they write things down to satisfy that need to express themselves, to be engaging with the world even when alone. That would make most writers extroverts, by standard definition. I would say that's way too simplistic – Steven Powers Chylinski describes himself as an introvert, drawing his energy from solitude rather than social interaction. Yet he has written a memoir that is both intimate and expansive, illuminating a soul who is very much a social animal, perhaps in spite of himself.

Dr. Powers Chylinski has achieved a delicate balance between describing his own life experiences while treading lightly on the stories and reputations of the people who inhabit his life narrative. Told in slice-of-life vignettes that span his life from childhood to middle age, his tales range from the sad to the bittersweet to the downright painful to the humorous. And he peppers them with fascinating asides about his distant ancestors whose lives he has researched for previous books.

One of Dr. Powers Chylinski's stated goals in writing this book was to discover his own identity in light of his life experiences and genealogical research. Answering the question *Who Am I?* leads to other queries – does our identity change over time? Do life experiences alter how we see ourselves? How, if at all, does knowing our ancestry change our self-assessment?

Interest in DNA testing and genetics has exploded in recent years as the technology becomes easily accessible to the public. In this massive world with its ever-growing population, the trend is for people to try to understand where they came from and to connect with the branches of their trees that have followed a different path. I hope readers will enjoy the stories of this professional researcher and identity-seeker, and be inspired to examine their own histories in order to answer essential questions about themselves.

Laura Lehner, MA, MLIS
Hudson, Ohio Library and Historical Society

Overview

There are several reasons why I am writing this memoir. One is to discover how, if at all, my sense of identity has changed as a result of both my life experiences and the discoveries I have made about my ancestors. I also want to trace the process by which I appointed myself the family story-teller. And, if by chance I should find the underlying reasons why I first began this investigative journey back decades ago, so much the better.

One facet of acquiring an identity is that as young children we hear various messages about ourselves from the important people in our lives from birth onward. Initially then, we leave it to others to tell us who we are. It is only later in our adolescent years, that we begin to acquire a core identity—an answer to the question, Who Am I?

What I do know about myself is that for the first twenty-five or more years of my life, I generally let others decide my identity and my sense of self-worth for me. And I am not a little embarrassed to admit this. After all, some psychological theories say that by the age of eighteen or so, the development of an identity ought to be mostly completed (Piaget, 1963).

However, for an increasing number of people, finding one's identity may also involve taking a broader, more inclusive view through family research. While such an effort is not common (yet), it is certainly another tool with which identity-seekers can gather additional data for their search of self.

> *Yet, supplementing one's identity through family research is not all fun and games. There are some potential hazards that might play havoc with a researcher's psyche. Terry Koch-Bostic, the director of the National Genealogical Society, says that roughly one in five genealogical researchers discover a negative surprise in their family tree. She adds, "We all find things that are really shocking and surprising."*

https://www.wsj.com/articles/SB10001424127887324734904578241822679163276 Retrieved 8/10/2017.

In a separate warning to more advanced genealogists--those who use DNA testing to confirm family relationships or sharpen their sense of identity--Megan Smolenyak Smolenyak says that DNA testing can help find "lost ethnic bloodlines that cross racial lines [which] can [in turn] challenge long-held assumptions about identity." Smolenyak's quotation is a repetition of Sue Shellenbarger's insights found in that same Wall Street Journal article cited above. In short, both Smolenyak and Shellenbarger believe that identity confusion may result for some individuals who take seriously the results of their DNA tests.

In any case, doing genealogical research is a fascinating way to discover one's roots and potentially to help clarify one's sense of identity. Whether we look only at the paper trail (documents pertaining to our family that can be found in libraries, courthouses, and more recently online) or if we dig deeper through DNA testing, family research offers interested parties a chance to refine their knowledge of who they are.

But for me, writing this autobiographical memoir also gives me a playing field on which to find how the events of my own life fit together. My memoir also allows me to leave something behind for future generations. Someone, somewhere in time may want to know who I was, what made me tick. And as an added benefit, I may glean what I get out of conducting family research. I am intrigued by the possibility that I do family research in the hope that I will discover more about myself, and especially about my motivations for appointing myself the family historian. Am I trying to feel better about myself? Am I attempting to overcome my inherent shyness? Do I hope to be loved by others if they know who I descend from? Intriguing questions all.

As for the text itself, I have changed nearly all of the names of the people and the names of many of the places cited in my work. I have made these alterations for obvious legal reasons. But just as importantly, I took seriously the words of memoirist Rosie Schaap in her book *Drinking With Men*. Ms. Schaap (2013) hints at the importance of protecting the reputations of the writer's fellow travelers when she says rather tersely, "The only person who should look like an asshole in your memoir is you." I believe I have thoroughly followed Schaap's advice about reporting my own perceptions of events, leaving it to readers to make their own judgments of the characters who inhabit my memoir. Here's hoping that I am the only person in my story that I have made to look foolish!

ACT ONE
Childhood

Scene 1: Eating dirty orange peels

From earliest childhood, I realized that I was a very shy person. I sometimes wonder if my shyness, which I considered a handicap, also acted as a motivator for me. I may have thought, "If I can overcome this handicap, I may actually achieve some successes, and in some way prove myself to be a worthwhile person—someone who was 'good enough.' " But I wonder now—"good enough" for what? Perhaps, I can answer this and other questions by examining some of my life experiences.

One of my first memories took place when I was four or five years old. It was the early 1950's, and still warm enough to be outside playing in short pants. I was new to the neighborhood, and in fact, new to the North. My family and I had just moved to the inner city of Cleveland from my mother's home in Kentucky. We had lived in Kentucky for but a few years after having lived in western Arkansas where I was born.

School had not yet started—in those days the school year did not begin until after the Labor Day holiday. My parents have told me that I spoke with a slow, meandering southern drawl compared with the mid-western faster-paced Cleveland accent. I sometimes wonder if people grew impatient waiting for me to finish my sentences peppered as they must have been with the slow cadence of my accent. Incidentally, many Clevelanders to this day believe that they have no discernible accents whatsoever. Take my word for it, they do.

I must have seemed like an anomaly to the neighborhood children on East 57th Street. After all, I was a smallish, shy, dark-skinned four or five-year-old who spoke English with strange inflections, and yet who had an identifiably-Polish last name. In fact, the entire neighborhood was a part of what is now called *Warszawa* (little Warsaw). In truth though, my street was populated not only by Poles, but by Germans, Welsh, Slovaks, and assorted others. Most of the men were employed either in the nearby steel mills or in other jobs requiring a strong back and a tolerance for heavy air and water pollution.

In the 1950s, Cleveland had several other Polish neighborhoods, in addition to the area of the city currently known as *Warszawa*. These areas included *Kantowa*, *Barberowa*, *Krakowa*, and *Poznan*. In each of these neighborhoods of the city there were bars, restaurants, grocery stores, bakeries, and even travel agencies, all catering to an enclave of Poles and Polish-Americans. From the 1890s to 1966, there were at least two Polish-language newspapers, including the *Wiadomosci Codzienne* (The Daily News) and the *Monitor Clevelandzki* (Cleveland Monitor). In short, my early years living in Cleveland were somewhat like living in a Polish village. I am not sure I fitted seamlessly into this environment.

Adding to the mix was the fact that at least for some time after I started kindergarten in the autumn, I had begun to stutter and to pull on my hair to the point that some of it would actually fall out! I suspect that my demeanor and personal habits helped some children in my new neighborhood to spot an easy target for merry-making. I remember that on one particular autumn day several older boys were sitting on the door stoop of the house diagonally across the street from mine. Noticing me, some of these children began to grin, and I believe they identified an opportunity for a good time.

This porch stoop was the setting for the "snack" of grimy orange peels.

Asking me to eat some dirty orange peels they had recently found on the ground, I obliged the boys by doing just that—ingesting a quantity of dirt-coated vitamin C. I may have even eaten every bit of the peels. I don't recall that specifically, but I do remember vividly the boys' laughter during my "meal." I was either too young or too frightened to know why they were laughing, but I believe I laughed with them. I have since told myself that I was simply too young to defend myself or even to know that the situation called for a defense.

The reality was that I was a bashful and frightened child—short, skinny, and ill-prepared for life in the big city. Yes, Cleveland was much bigger then than now. In the 1950 U.S. Census, the city itself had a population of nearly one million, and that does not include the several hundred thousand other souls who resided in the outlying suburbs of Cuyahoga County.

It was also a very dirty city. Pittsburghers are fond of citing the black specks of particulates that settled on their cars every morning during the 1950s and 1960s. Cleveland had its own version of solidified environmental hazards. But unlike Pittsburgh's, Cleveland's was red. The sky was often filled with a reddish glow that could be seen from all over Cleveland's east side. The atmospheric filth made for some unique and strangely beautiful sunsets, but who knows what damage it did to the residents of *Krakowa*, *Poznan*, and *Warszawa* (east side ethnic enclaves all) as well as other parts of the eastern half of the city.

And of course who could forget the stories on the national news about the fire on Cleveland's oil-slicked Cuyahoga River on June 22, 1969. As river fires go, the 1969 blaze was little more than a campfire that caused a mere $50,000 in damage. At least 13 blazing fires have been reported on the Cuyahoga since the first in 1868. The most destructive of the fires took place in 1952. That one produced a staggering one million dollars in damage. Thankfully, both the Ohio Environmental Protection Agency and its Federal counterpart have seen fit to help Cleveland to help the river recover. To a large degree, the river now supports both recreation and healthy aquatic life. A 2007 survey of the river's health by Kent State University has shown that at least in the middle reaches of that body of water "… in and near Kent, [the Cuyahoga River] is in FULL attainment for aquatic life." Found in the Cuyahoga now are fish such as northern hogsuckers, rock bass, northern pike, and smallmouth bass. (https://kentohio.net/kent-alive/cuyahoga-river-after-the-flames Retrieved 11/22/2017.)

But alas, a cleaner river and healthier atmosphere do not make a little boy less bashful or more confident. I sometimes sought solace and safety in books. Learning to read was a godsend to me. I can vividly recall the arrival of the bookmobile, an RV-like bus outfitted with shelves, and looking very much the same as the interior of the neighborhood library. And perhaps prophetically, it was the biographies that drew my attention most often.

The bookmobile carried a series of orange, hard-covered bios about famous historical characters. I felt so excited reading about the exploits and adventures of Abraham Lincoln, Davey Crockett, George Washington, and Daniel Boone, a fellow Kentuckian (Kentucky was Boone's adopted home territory). I never would have guessed so many decades ago that in my family research, I would discover a Daniel Boone connection.

> *In 1778, Daniel Boone led a party of salt-gatherers to the Licking River near a frontier fort in central Kentucky. Boone was captured by a band of Shawnee warriors, and marched with nearly all of his men back to the village they called Little Chillicothe in the modern state of Ohio, where he and Joseph Josiah Jackson were adopted by the Shawnee.*
>
> *It was the custom of the Shawnee to adopt men (race was not a barrier to adoption) to replace warriors who had been killed in battle. Both Boone and Jackson were not only adopted by the tribe, but they must have felt quite at home with the Shawnee for they voluntarily stayed with them for a year of more. Joseph Josiah Jackson (1756-1844), a veteran of the American Revolutionary War, was my seventh great-grandfather. One circle closes.*
>
> *Even George Washington entered the Underwood/Powers/Chylinski family history. It seems that in March 1774, Lieutenant George pleaded for his first military promotion from Colonel Richard Corbin, my eighth great-grandfather. In response to Washington's plea for a military promotion, Corbin wrote back to the then-lieutenant, "Dear George: I enclose you your commission. God prosper you with it. [signed] Your friend, Richard Corbin." Theodore J. Crackell ed. (2007). The papers of George Washington, Digital Edition. Charlottesville, VA: University of Virginia Press. Retrieved 12/23/2014.*

But, reflecting again on my early years, I have come to realize that so many of my childhood memories have centered on my demeanor as a quiet, shy, studious youngster. I loved learning, books, the outdoors, and generally the quiet life. And if I chose to do so, I felt and still feel, quite comfortable being alone for a time.

Scene 2: There goes the ankle

When I was about ten years old, I was playing—probably baseball—at Warsaw Park, a city-owned playground and baseball field at the corner of East 64th Street and Harvard Avenue in Cleveland.

I don't remember the details clearly, but I had just hurt my (right?) foot so that it began to swell badly. Who knows, it may even have been fractured. I recall feeling helpless, although I was only about 10 city blocks from my home on East 57th Street, just off Harvard.

Yet, I could barely walk and my foot seemed to be swelling more and more by the minute. I was at a loss about what to do to get help. But, soon I spotted the parking lot of the Kroger store at the top of a nearby grassy knoll. There were Kroger Stores in Cleveland in those days, though they disappeared in the mid-1980s once its Solon, Ohio plant closed due to high labor costs.

I had hoped to ask someone—even a stranger—to drive me back to my place of safety at the southern end of East 57th. It seems that "stranger danger" was not a popular phrase issued by worried parents to protect their children in the 1950s. I am not sure if people were less aware of the negative possibilities of children's interactions with strange adults or if the world (that is, my Midwestern world) was simply a safer place in the mid-twentieth century.

I knew my mother would be at home, puttering around the house doing her daily chores. I am not sure what I hoped she could do for me, except to give me comfort. She did not know how to drive, and even if she did, she had no car. Somehow though, I believed she would rescue me.

Not having money for a pay telephone to call for my mother at our easy-to-remember home number--Vulcan 3-1971--I just hobbled up the knoll to the supermarket. There, I found a neighbor—Mr. Twarzinski—who lived across the street and a few houses to the north of my own house. Surely, he would help me. He had a light green '57 Plymouth, the one with the huge tail fins, and it would be a simple matter for him to cart me off to my house. But, lo and behold, Mr. Twarzinski refused to drive me anywhere. I was shocked! Weren't all grown-ups like Mom and Dad—having my best interests at heart? The answer, apparently, was a resounding "NO!"

Now, what was I to do? My friends were no help since they did not drive, and they had no money for a pay telephone call either. And in any case, I don't remember them even being at Warsaw playground that day. Sometimes, I just wangled my way into a ball game, even when strangers were playing. I loved the game so much that occasionally I swallowed my great reticence, and asked just anyone if I could join their game.

No, I was on my own now. My father was at work, and my mother could be no help even if I could have telephoned her. Besides, Mom was at least as shy as I was. I could not picture her going from house to house to seek help for me from some other neighbor.

Stranded away from home and help, I made a decision that I only now realize was an important one—I would take care of myself. I decided to limp home on my wounded body part. Somehow, I would make it! I don't recall the details of my walk—but I do remember how much my ankle hurt, how my shoe barely fit my swollen foot, and how very long it took me to navigate those few blocks.

With the gift of hindsight, I suppose I learned three life lessons from this experience: First, I came to understand that all adults (and children too?) are not necessarily interested in helping me. Secondly, I discovered that people are sometimes so engrossed in their own issues that they forget that others have needs too. I later learned that Mr. Twarzinski physically abused his wife and children, and that his wife had children by another man while she was still married to Mr. T. In fact, those children came into the world with serious birth defects. Finally, and perhaps most importantly, I learned that sometimes the only one I can count on is me! I am still trying to reinforce that last life lesson—it is not an easy one for me to accept.

Scene 3: Mom and Dad tell me who I am

In spite of or perhaps even because of my shyness, I just loved being a student, and I cherished so many of my teachers. Beginning with my first experiences in school, I have been drawn to quality teachers and to quality teaching. To name just a few, there was Mrs. Clark, Mrs. Fleiger, Mrs. Lahlebach, Mr. Wolfe, and Sister Margaret Thomas. Each of them played a major part in my love of learning. They are all deceased now, and I never told any of them how much they meant to me and to the new "me" I was becoming. How very much they each influenced me! I have been so fortunate to have met and been inspired by these classroom role models!

And because of their influence, I could not have chosen a more appropriate occupation for myself than teaching as my life's work. During my work life, I can only hope that I did for others what my teachers did for me—opened the door to knowledge and perhaps to wisdom.

In his stirring article, "The Heart of the Teacher: Identity and Integrity in Teaching," Parker J. Palmer commented that "Teaching holds a mirror to the soul. If I am willing to look in that mirror, and not run from what I see, I have a chance to gain self-knowledge— and knowing myself is as crucial to good teaching as knowing my students and my subject" (1991, p.1). Palmer continues, "We became teachers for reasons of the heart, animated by a passion for some subject and for helping people to learn" (p.6). Sage words, indeed. If my early teachers had heard Palmer's inspiring words, I believe they would have heartily agreed with them!

It is obvious to me that my later behaviors were based on the values I acquired in school and at home. Growing up, my values were my parents' values—attend church every Sunday, go to Confession every few weeks to ask for forgiveness, follow the Ten Commandments, and try to be perfect (at least that was my childhood interpretation of their/our values).

Attending public schools, I was required to go to Confraternity of Christian Doctrine (also known as "CCD") classes, the Catholic equivalent of Sunday school. The task there mainly consisted of memorizing the Church's *Baltimore Catechism*. For example, "Steven: Why did God make you?" My answer: "God made me to know, love, and serve Him in this world and to be happy with Him forever in the next." And you had better give that exact answer, or else… beware. Those stories about nuns using a ruler across a student's knuckles are not always fabrications.

I suppose the CCD classes must have been successful since I made my first Confession (the sacrament of Penance) in a timely way, and in my beautiful, sweet, childhood innocence and holiness, made my First Communion (the Sacrament of the Eucharist) at the age of eight or nine. I remember feeling proud and grown up after completing my First Communion.

The author on his First Communion day

It was traditional, and perhaps it still is, to give the First Communicant money, and some sort of congratulatory card—Hallmark makes a wide variety of these cards to this day. I had expected to get lots of money (maybe as much as hundreds of dollars). But, I was disappointed. Being from a poor family living in a poor, inner city neighborhood, with only poor relatives, my "take" was also poor. I received little or no money for this auspicious occasion. My desire for money was, of course, a value in itself.

A typical First Communion card from the 1950s

In childhood and in early adolescence, I also valued being a good baseball player, as well as being one of the fastest runners in my neighborhood. As much as I *liked* to run, I *loved* baseball. I loved it so much that I wanted to become a professional, that is, a major league player like my childhood heroes. In fact, I often played two or three, nine-inning baseball games per day. I either never got physically tired or at least I never realized that I should have been exhausted. No wonder I slept so well in those early days.

I played sports so often that my parents sometimes punished me for being outside too much. How different the world has become. Kids now need to be begged to turn off their electronics, and to go outside to play. Today, punishment often consists in having one's electronic toys taken away for a period of time.

As an adult, my values have changed. For example, I no longer follow the Church's dictates simply because I have to do so for fear of being struck down if I fail to follow the exact "letter of the law." This shift may even show in my current physical appearance. I no longer have the look of that eight or nine-year-old who stares back at me with that sweet and innocent face from the aging black and white photographs that were taken at my First Communion.

Instead, my values seem deeper, more genuine, and are an integral part of the person I have become. For example, just a few months ago, I began a conversation with a person who was standing in line behind me at an airport while waiting to board a flight. It seems the stranger worked for the same organization as my wife, but at a different physical location.

After she told me her occupation and the reason for her business travel, I told the woman that my wife worked for the same employer as she did. Still, I did not tell her my wife's name. Lo and behold! The stranger later off-handedly told one of my wife's coworkers about her meeting the husband of a fellow employee. The stranger then proceeded to tell the co-worker what a kind man she had met at the airport.

Yet, we had spoken so very little and for such a short time while standing in line. Apparently, I have at least occasionally incorporated the value of kindness to strangers (and to others, I hope) into my behavior. I seem to do so without consciously deciding to be kind. Repeating this airport experience is not intended as a boast. Rather, it is to remind *myself* that I don't have to accept my parents' values or the Church's dictates uncritically, but that over time, I have developed and cherished my own.

Scene 4: Graduating Harvard, Going to Mars

Of course, values also help to determine the plans for all of us for the future—our hopes and dreams for what we want to become during our time on earth. For some fortunate few who have an early-identified "mission" that is, a direction for their life's work, their hopes and dreams often have a way of coming true.

My own hopes and dreams have changed over time. Between the start of my school career at age 5, and near the end of my high school tenure, I thought of at least four separate careers for my future, all of which reflect my then-current values. For example, in the 4th, 5th, and 6th grades I dreamed of becoming an astronomer. Of course, at that age, I had no idea what astronomers actually did, other than look at the stars through a telescope. I had no sense of the training it took, where to get the training, or if I could muster the requisite skills or abilities to do that work.

At my sixth grade graduation from Harvard—yes, I did graduate from Harvard (Elementary School, that is)—I must have told someone about my career hopes as some school authority figure (either a teacher or the school principal, Mrs. Markowitz) read not only my name to the assembled audience, but added, "Steve likes to look upon the stars; And we predict he'll go to Mars." What optimism!

Later, in junior high and perhaps in the early years of high school, I dreamed of becoming a professional baseball player. Next, I contemplated a career as a veterinarian, and then as a priest. Yet, I knew nothing of the requirements for entering those fields, and I did nothing to obtain that information.

The truth is I had virtually no guidance on potential careers or on much of anything from my parents. I am not blaming my parents for their lack of guidance. In reality, both my mother and father were undereducated—talented, but unschooled. They could be little help as my mentors even if they wanted to do so.

Scene 5: The Bashful Kid and the Spelling Bee

Years before I made any firm decisions about the direction of my life, I was able to reach a few personal milestones. To achieve these markers, I had to partially overcome my shyness, become more assertive and less socially backward. Entering spelling contests, completing school projects, and playing neighborhood baseball games were all venues for these milestones. Yet, given my shortcomings, I could not have predicted these successes.

For example with the gift of hindsight, I now realize that I probably started my school career too early. In turn, this early start to school may have contributed to my uneasiness in social settings. My birthday is in August, and the cut-off day for entering kindergarten in the Cleveland Public Schools was about August 31 of each school year. In other words, most of my classmates then and throughout my school career were as much as a whole year older than I was.

Certainly my compatriots' age advantage showed socially in my hesitant interactions with my classmates. In fact, I do not recall a single school friend or acquaintance when I was in kindergarten or even when I entered the first grade. My behavior seems to fit with some of the research on shyness.

Jerome Kagan, a researcher at Harvard University, has studied the genetic roots of shyness extensively. He believes that as many as 10% to 15% of all children are born shy. As toddlers, these children often become fearful and behaviorally inhibited. They tend to remain quiet, cautious and introverted in elementary school. In adolescence, they have significantly higher rates of social anxiety, that is, they become somewhat more nervous in social situations. The children Kagan studied all had elevated resting heart rates, and generally their parents had increased rates of social anxiety disorder (SAD), an American Psychological Association clinical diagnosis. All of this evidence suggests that shyness likely has genetic causes.

But academically, my bashful behavior seemed to drift into the background. For example, the earliest milestone I can recall took place when I was nine years old. I became the spelling champion of my school's fourth grade class. I won that distinction during the school's spelling "bee".

> *OK, here I will admit to being a bit of a nerd when it comes to the etymology of words and phrases. In writing this memoir, I confess that I googled the phrase, spelling bee. It seems the word "bee" may come from the Middle English word, bene, meaning a favor or a prayer.*
> http://spellingbee.com/origin-term-spelling-bee. Retrieved 12/8/2017.

In any case, spelling contests were originated by the *Louisville Courier Journal* in 1925. Today, such contests are held in countries as diverse as Nigeria, India, Abu Dhabi, Dubai, Australia, Bangladesh, Kuwait, Nepal, and of course the United States.

As for my own experiences, I repeated my spelling achievement in the fifth grade, and in fact, I was the spelling champion of the entire school that year. I was even allowed to enter the city-wide spelling championship that was sponsored by the *Cleveland Press*.

Although I did not get far in that competition, I count even that success as a milestone in my academic career. The word that tripped me up, forcing my early exit from the competition was—*geranium*. I no longer misspell that tricky word.

The author in "Hopalong Cassidy" western garb, his sister Sharon, his paternal grandmother Stella, and his father Steve J. Chylinski (from left to right)

Scene 6: Dogs, babies, birds, Buddy & Brian

They liked me, animals and children. They still do. I recall reading several studies in a social psychology textbook that babies and children seem to prefer people with proportional faces. Ears, eyes, mouths that all fit with one another appear to attract the attention of babies and children, more than those features that do not quite fit.

So perhaps the reason that children are drawn to me is something out of my control--the face I was born with. Or perhaps, I simply like children, and I smile at them as I rejoice in the possibilities of these new, hopeful, young lives. They often return my smile, and our eyes meet. Still, maybe they seem to like me because I became a teacher? Could babies and children tell my occupation by simply looking at me? I doubt it.

As for dogs, I cannot say why they seem interested in me. Recently meeting my son's young German shepherd for the first time, I was struck by how she seemed to want my attention. She followed me around his house, from one room to another. Yet, she followed no one else. Then, when I turned my back on her, she bumped into my backside several times until I turned to pet her and talk to her. Go figure! I have loved animals, especially dogs, since I was a little boy. Yet, dogs were not my only pets.

As an eight or ten-year-old, I found a baby sparrow in my back yard. I took the bird into my house in the inner city of Cleveland so I could care for him/her (how do you tell a sparrow's gender?). I loved that formerly wild bird. I called it "Tweetie." Not an original name, but an easy one to remember. I would take my bird outside, and he/she would fly into the nearest tree. Extending my index finger, Tweetie would immediately fly from the tree and land on my finger. I can still feel how warm his/her body felt against my skin.

Some years later, I also had a robin for a pet. "Robbie" stayed with me at night, and hung around with me outside when I went in the yard to play. I did not have Robbie for long, as he/she simply disappeared one day. An exhaustive search of the house produced the bird's wet and lifeless body. He/she had met his/her end in the toilet. Robbie was a non-swimmer.

Puddles and author (front), sisters Rita and Sharon (back)

Yet, it was dogs that garnered most of my attention. I can still recall the names of the various pet dogs I had as a child. There were Princess and Bubbles, a mother-daughter team. We were not able to sell or even give away Bubbles, the puppy. Finding no takers, we simply kept the young dog.

Then there was Puddles, my beloved cocker spaniel. It is probably easy to guess how Puddles earned his name. He fought toilet training with great energy. Had Puddles been a human being in Sigmund Freud's day, the two of them would have had marvelous conversations that would have been recorded in psychology textbooks, and read by budding mental health professionals to this day.

When he was hit by a car (Puddles, not Freud), I cried deeply and longingly for my friend, the black cocker, for days on end. My human friends thought it was funny that I mourned the loss of a mere dog. I never understood their laughter. A friend lost is a friend lost, no matter if he was a canine or not.

Sometimes, friendships are lost even before they begin to solidify. There were Buddy Matchek and Brian LaPlage, who were both neighbors and would-be friends who lived near my East 57th Street house. What is noteworthy about these two characters is that they almost never seemed to like me. While I very much wanted them to be my friends, they often conspired in some way to leave me out of their duo. At times, they would act interested in being friends with me, then just as quickly, we would be on the "outs." I never knew why. In turn, I am not sure why the friendship of these two boys was important to me, but it was. Although I had other friends on that street, I so craved the friendship of Brian and Buddy, too.

Only Buddy is alive today. Still, I had heard a rumor that he had died some years ago. Searching through the web site, www.ancestry.com, I discovered that it was Buddy's brother, Larry, who had died. Presumably, Buddy is still alive and perhaps even well. We never did become friends. In at least one other way, the Matchek boys were also my entrepreneurial competition. Together, the brothers delivered the *Wiadomosci Codzienne*, a Polish-language rival to my *Cleveland Press* paper route. We vied for some of the same customers, creating a new reason to remain non-friends.

As for Brian, he obsessed about trucks--the big rigs that hauled trailers around. He and Richard Schmidt, another nearby resident, shuttled around the neighborhood on their bicycles making roaring sounds like a truck that had lost its brakes on a steep, downward-tilting hill. At that same genealogical web site, I discovered that Brian died in 2005 in a private home while living in zip code 44105--our old zip. Perhaps, since the record shows he died at home, he may have passed away in his original childhood house. Still other records show that Richard, a military veteran, died in 1976, while he was still a very young man. I could find no cause for his death in those documents.

I have generally recovered from my lack of friendship with Brian. I see him now as a mere former acquaintance. But his sister, Sharon, was another story. She was one of my first love objects—a girl at least five or six years older than me. She was aloof, and seldom came out of her house—I should know since I often waited near her house hoping she would appear. I wonder whatever happened to Sharon. She sure was a beauty!

As for actual friends in my inner city Cleveland neighborhood, the first were Artie and Mickey. I sometimes wonder why in the 1950s (and perhaps this is still true in the 21st century), the names given to the friends of young children so often ended in the "y" or "ie" sound. There must be some psychological or sociological reason for this tradition, but its genesis escapes me.

It pleases me to recall summer evenings with these two friends as we played imaginative games for hours on end, became cowboys and Indians while wearing our cute western or tribal outfits, and sometimes catching fireflies only to have them die by the next morning following their night spent in cleansed *Kraft* mayonnaise jar. The container's lid always had several perforations designed to forestall the deaths of our insect friends. My very favorite game, which could involve dozens of neighborhood children, was hide-and-seek. The area felt so safe that parents allowed the game to go on until late in the evening, well past twilight. Were neighborhoods truly safer then, or were parents and children simply more ignorant about life's pitfalls?

Scene 7: Mamaw & me down by the White Castle®

It seems that in my childhood, a few select relatives felt like friends in some strange way. For instance, I knew that my maternal grandmother Mary Underwood Powers loved me. I am convinced of that. Whereas my mother probably loved me, I do not recall ever hearing her say she did, unless I first told her I loved her. "Mamaw", on the other hand, was this warm, wide, wonderful teddy-bear of a person. The entire time I knew her, her hair was as white as a Midwestern snowfall. She was also overweight, and most importantly, she was extremely kind and loving.

The unfortunate fact however, was that she lived nearly four hundred miles away from me in Kentucky. And in the 1950s, she might as well have lived across the continent. There were no interstate highways back then—Dwight D. Eisenhower's dream of a cross-country road system was only a distant hope. No, it was old U.S. Route 42—called Pearl Road in Cleveland, and Brownsboro Road in Louisville—that supported our old General Motors' vehicles the entire distance between those cities. Regardless or its name, that Cleveland to Louisville thoroughfare was a two-lane road—one lane in each direction.

The trip from Cleveland to Louisville by car took at least twelve hours, that is, if there was no fog along the Ohio River. On some of those foggy nights, we could count on an extra three or four hours of travel time. Besides, have you ever tried to take a long-distance trip in a used, non-air conditioned 1952 Chevrolet? It was not the ideal way to travel with two adults and three children. And, it was always a Chevrolet that our family used for its trips to Kentucky. Not only did my father work for General Motors for a substantial part of his working life, but he frowned upon any vehicle manufactured by Ford or others. Further, he downright loathed any car made by the Chrysler Corporation. For Chrysler products he reserved a special epithet. On numerous occasions, he was heard to blurt out (in mixed company or not), "I wouldn't hit a dog in the ass with a Chrysler product." That statement was also the source of much giggling in the back seat of the Louisville-bound Chevy.

We were always getting on the nerves of the others in the car. Dad had a solution to the cramped quarters—we would stop at every *White Castle®* restaurant he could find between Cleveland and central Kentucky. I can still hear him bellow to the server at that venerable old chain of fast food restaurants (their slogan: "Buy 'em by the sack!"). And at the low, low cost of ten cents per burger, we could afford dozens of them at every stop.

"Gimme three dozen *white castles*, without cheese." He had a smile on his face when he said this. And the clerk would respond with something like:

"Yessir! Three dozen 'a them little beauties comin' up. You must either have a massive appetite or you have quite a clan." Dad would respond to this opening with:

"Yep, there are five of us, and we are hungry as hell." Dad liked to swear. On later trips, the number of the family members would change, as more babies were born. Dad would take these opportunities to proudly announce the change in our population. "… there are six of us… seven of us… eight of us… nine of us… ten of us (ultimately, eight children and Mom and Dad)."

But, once we arrived in Louisville--that smelly old cow town, for Mamaw lived on Story Avenue near the stockyards and the Oertel's Brewery—it was non-stop love and kindness from my venerable old grandmother. "Want a good meal—here have some," she would say. "Want some money to get an ice cream cone at Meyer's Drug Store---here's a little change, go on up there!"

The stockyards' smell and the aroma of the hops roasting at Oertel's are not the only smells locked into my memory. There was also the aroma drifting from Grandpa Powers' musty old barn on the rear of the property. And if you were really fortunate, there was the early morning smell of warm bread baking at Hellmueller's Bakery located across the alley just beyond the barn. Although Hellmueller's was located on Washington Avenue, the rear of the building faced the Powers' barn. I can still experience those wonderful aromas. These olfactory memories remind me so much of sweeter days, and of the love and tenderness exuding from my maternal grandparents that I am lifted back in time.

The smell of Grandpa Powers' pipe tobacco burning in the house on Story Avenue is still present with me as if that odor was wafting past my nose at this very minute. Finally, there was the aroma emanating from the little white bag of good Kentucky tobacco that Grandpa carried in his pocket for appropriate occasions (which were often). When he was not "rolling his own" (cigarettes, that is), he was gingerly stuffing tobacco into his pipe. I still have that pipe where it is lovingly stored in a drawer of my desk. It is the only memento I have from my Papaw's life. Occasionally, I retrieve the Powers' pipe and suck in that tobacco smell that remains half a century later. It is my way of immortalizing Papaw!

What experiences I had in the American South! I had lots of free time since I was typically on a summer break, and I had only to ask for something, and my childish wish would either be granted or at least a viable alternative would be offered. What great memories! Years later, I have come to believe that it was because of my grandmother that I began to collect family stories. I think story-collecting and story-telling may be ways in which I honor and even keep alive those long-gone days.

For example, it was my grandmother who tipped me off about the family graveyard at the top of the hill across the street from the parking lot of the Jackson Picnic Area of Bernheim Forest and Arboretum in Bullitt County, Kentucky. On a warm spring day in the late 1960s, Mamaw, my mother, and my maternal uncle James all piled out of James' Chevy with its throaty 427 cubic inch engine, and headed for the nearby, heavily wooded and very steep hill. Our destination, the Jackson family cemetery, was located just at the top of the ridge of that hill.

On the way up, Grandma Powers pointed out the area in which she had lived beginning in 1902. The cabin, now long gone and a victim of the ravages of time had belonged to her grandfather Eli Underwood (1849-1942). Perhaps, the cabin and surrounding land had even earlier belonged to Eli's father, Willis Underwood (1807-1911). Yes, Willis' date of death is correct. In fact, family lore has him dying by falling off his horse at age 104.

> *Lying in the nineteenth century burying ground are John T. Jackson (1839-1926) and his consort, my great grandmother, Rose Ann Jones (1864-1940). Jackson was a Union veteran of the American Civil War. Ironically, his own father, John Thomas Jackson (1803/1812-1863) was a Confederate cavalryman under the leadership of General John Hunt Morgan. I can only imagine what the dinner conversations were like between the Yankee son and his Rebel father. The elder Jackson was captured by Union troops in Bullitt County, Kentucky and transported to the Fort Delaware prison where he died only a few months after his initial imprisonment. Due to frequent spring flooding, his remains and those of his Rebel comrades were moved to a new site in New Jersey. His body was never returned to his beloved Kentucky. John Thomas's widow, Catherine Spencer Jackson (1806-1904), would not have the privilege of lying next to her husband. Instead she is buried in the Snyder Family Cemetery in Hancock County, Kentucky near her daughter Celia, and her son-in-law. The Jackson couple lay 754 miles apart for eternity. How unfair life often seems.*

As for Grandma Underwood Powers' historical astuteness, she was simply a wealth of information about her distant family, at least for the previous three generations. She could and sometimes did regale me for hours with her tales of the family's life in the Kentucky hills. Although I had begun to formally research her/our forebears in the early 1970s, Mamaw was quick to correct any misinformation I assumed was accurate. In a paraphrase of an old English proverb, there was no way I could "teach Grandma how to suck eggs." As a septuagenarian who had led a colorful and engaging life, she was already familiar with egg-sucking.

Scene 8: Mama, me, and alcoholism

Yet, in spite of knowing that my maternal grandmother loved me, I remain confused to this day about my mother's love and indeed about her behavior in general. Certainly, my mother was not mean or cruel in any way. As a child, I simply accepted her quiet, unassuming demeanor as the way she was. I don't recall expecting any more than her demure presence.

So, I was shocked when I learned that not all mothers were so quiet and so unassertive. I do not know exactly when this realization took place, but it certainly did. I recall once telling her that I wanted to know her better—that is how invisible she seemed to me at times. Her response also surprised me as she said "There isn't much to know!" I did not say it at the time, but looking back on that very brief conversation, it seems to me that my mother had a terrible self-image. I also have wondered about her childhood experiences. What were her early years like? How was she treated by her mother? Or by her father or by her siblings for that matter?

She was intelligent and well-spoken except for such American Southernisms as, "That boy was buck-necked" (translation: the boy had no clothes on). Getting any information from her about her childhood, her parents or her grandparents was nearly always a struggle. Maybe I ought to have been more patient with her—waiting longer for her answers, and pursuing every "I don't know" or "We were just like everyone else" more aggressively.

And now, it is too late. She died in March 2012. She passed away just as she had lived, slipping quietly away in the middle of the night with no one special present. Her caregiver said she took a final deep breath, and then suddenly she was gone. As luck would have it, I was in an aircraft flying at 35,000 feet somewhere near Chicago on my way to see my daughter in Arizona when my mother died.

I never did get to say good-bye to her. In fact, we had to delay her wake and burial until I returned to Ohio. During the last few years of her life, she developed a slowly-advancing, but personality-eroding case of dementia. I cannot tell you the number of times she inquired about my father who had died the previous year. "Where is your father? Did he die?" Patiently, I answered her questions each time she would ask, perhaps as many as five or six times in a single hour.

I suppose she influenced me and inadvertently promoted my own shyness, and my non-assertive, quiet nature. After all, I spent so many hours with this bashful, introverted woman prior to finding my own voice. Perhaps, beginning in adolescence, I felt forced to "rise above" or go beyond my own learned or innate tendencies toward shyness and social backwardness.

Rarely did I see my mother escape into her inner world of emotions, personal beliefs, and or watch her assert herself. One of those unique emotional occasions occurred during a particular bout of my father's heavy drinking. I was about ten years old and I was sitting quietly in a room in the house on East 57th Street. My mother was also there, ironing a large stack of clothes. Quite suddenly and uncharacteristically, my mother began to cry, almost to sob, blurting out these words, "I don't know what to do about him. I think I should get out of here! Leave him [your father] for good."

Now, what does a ten-year-old say to something like that? I can only imagine how she must have suffered because of my father's drinking. Yet, she seemed to have no one to turn to for support, no confidante. I am not sure there were support systems like Al-Anon for relatives of alcoholics in those days. Nor am I convinced that she would have attended such help groups even if such support existed.

One of the many difficulties engendered by this degenerative disease of alcoholism is that the habitual drinker is so enamored with and addicted to alcohol that he/she thinks about virtually nothing else except where the next drink is coming from. And the physical and/or emotional absence of the alcoholic leaves others to face the results of the drinking—unpaid bills, dunning telephone calls from bill collectors, and a shortage of funds with which to buy food or other necessities.

At times, it seemed the telephone would not stop ringing. My mother, never one to respond quickly to anything, would mutter some excuse for the lack of bill payments. Her life must have been exceptionally difficult during those days of heavy drinking and unpaid debts. She never did leave my father, but certainly she had reasons aplenty for doing so.

Scene 9: Pica and a security blanket

I have tried to analyze what coping mechanisms I used to survive my childhood. Having an alcoholic father and a bashful, self-deprecating mother made my life difficult to say the least. Further, I had a slew of younger siblings—some much younger. Being the first born of eight children, I found still another set of challenges. As the oldest, I was sometimes asked to change diapers, make some meals on my own, and learn to darn my socks and other such chores. All this left me with a sense that I was on my own and in danger of being set adrift to fend for myself. Here, I don't intend to garner sympathy for myself, but at times I thought I needed more attention and support. Perhaps that is the bane of all first-borns in families that have many children.

This sounds like a situation for a Linus-like security blanket like the character from the Peanuts cartoon. In my memory, I can recall having no literal security blanket or security object when I was a child. However, I now know that I may have had an undiagnosed case of *pica* as a child. Pica is the condition, often triggered by a nutritional deficiency or by an anxiety-producing situation, in which the victim eats some non-food object as a source of nutritional-replacement or anxiety-reduction. In my case, a physician, had I seen one, could have diagnosed me with *papyrophagia*—ingesting paper.

Blinder and Salama (2008), in their article, "An update on pica: Prevalence, contributing causes, and treatment," believe that pica is linked to stressors such as family issues, maternal deprivation, emotional trauma, parental neglect, a disorganized family structure, or in the case of a woman, pregnancy. https://en.wikipedia.org/wiki/Pica_(disorder). Retrieved 10/20/2016. According to another study by Sayetta (1986), the material eaten often contains a mineral that the person diagnosed with pica needs.

Testing for the presence of pica is suggested for people who are malnourished or who have lower than normal nutrient intake. For others, a diagnosis of pica can be accompanied by a need for social attention. Certainly, a child who wants to gain more notice from her/his parents could do so by eating a non-nutritional substance in front of them.

I do not know how long my pica-like behavior lasted. As a grown-up clinical counselor, I learned that the condition is not uncommon in small children (15% to 75%) or pregnant women (8% to 74%), and that it must persist for more than a month for an accurate diagnosis to be made. I was quite young when this behavior began, so I have little memory of the details.

Yet, I can still recall the pungent taste of a fresh slice of the *Cleveland Press* newspaper. I suppose I should have seen our family doctor, Vitus Pekaric, but that would have been inconvenient and costly. Unless we were actually looking half-dead and writhing on the floor, unable to stand, we Chylinskis seldom sought medical care. A suspected case of pica hardly would qualify as a near-death experience in our family.

ACT TWO
Adolescence

Scene 1: Poverty, hunger, and the "Butcher"

I was so naïve, I thought it was perfectly normal that members of my family of origin had to slither up to the "Butcher's" to ask for food. Thanks in large part to my father's drinking, my family had little or nothing to eat at times, and certainly little or no money with which to buy food. Mr. and Mrs. Rozitski, both Polish immigrants, owned a small neighborhood grocery store on the south side of Harvard Avenue between East 57th and East 59th Streets in Cleveland. Mr. Rozitski was known in the neighborhood simply as "the Butcher." Besides selling commercially-prepared food, Mr. Rozitski also used his sharp knives and cleavers to trim fat from larger chunks of meat, carving them into steaks, chops, and other cuts.

Now the "Butcher" and his wife lived in the rear of the shop, and had a small apartment on their building's second floor. My mother and several of my siblings and I would sheepishly knock on their door after hours, and then ask the couple to retrieve groceries from their shop. Either the Butcher or his wife would kindly give us supplies enough to survive, while accepting our word that we would pay for the food at a later date.

I am not sure we ever repaid the Rozitskis for their kindness and generosity. Nor do I recall feeling embarrassed or ashamed that we had no food in our house. It seems that I simply accepted our plight since I knew of no other way to live except to function in poverty and with bottles of beer and alcohol hidden not-so-discretely around the house.

What a surprise it was to find out that other fathers were sober most of the time. Some fathers were likely sober all the time. As children, my sisters and I suffered through considerable deprivation. For many years, my father used our scant money supplies to buy booze. My memory, perhaps faulty, is that I seldom had enough to eat. To this day, I generally eat more quickly than anyone else at the table. Might I be in a hurry to finish a meal lest someone take from me the necessary calories and nutrition?

While my mother struggled to find ways to feed her growing family, my father was typically out drinking or asleep, so it was almost exclusively my mother who cared for my family of origin. Finally, my father quit his supervisory job at General Motors, perhaps in a fit of impatience or in a drunken stupor. I am not sure how old I was when my father changed our lives for the worse by leaving his job, but I was old enough to know that the change meant trouble for the family.

It was so very difficult for me to live with the uncertainty that alcohol addiction created in my family. I am not sure what this tale has to do with my mission as family historian. Perhaps, suffering makes me a better writer. I don't know. I do suspect that I am much more empathetic and sympathetic toward people than I would have been otherwise. Still another answer could be that living through the difficult times has allowed me to identify with the difficult lives that many of my ancestors led.

There was a period in history when life expectancy was in the 20s or early 30s, a time when children often died, if not at the time of their birth, then soon after. Often, it was the mother who had just delivered who died in childbirth or shortly afterwards. Husbands were then left to raise the children on their own or to quickly remarry if they wanted help in raising their children. Romantic love was seldom a consideration with these first or second marriages. Further, disease, death, suffering, and disappointment ran rampant in the past. To a large degree, those four factors still plague many families and individuals worldwide.

I don't mean to suggest that I can accurately compare my childhood with the lives of my ancestors that lived through famines, plagues, infant deaths, starvation, early death, wars, and other calamities. Yet, it is with a certain sympathy that I read about their stories, identifying to a degree with their troubles, and in a vicarious way, I feel close to them. They are not just names from the fifth through the sixteenth centuries. But, rather they are human beings with whom I share a limited amount of DNA, and some of the woes that *homo sapiens* has suffered through time. They are my flesh and blood.

In my own case, my father finally stopped drinking when I was about 19 or twenty years old. He never took another drink in his life that I am aware of. One of the steps in the Alcoholics Anonymous' 12-step program is to attempt to make "restitution" for the hurt that the recovering alcoholic has caused through his/her behavior. I believe my father tried to do just that during the final thirty years of his life. I am not sure how one makes up for contributing to decades of suffering, but I do know my father attempted to make amends for his behavior.

Following my father's departure from General Motors, he worked as a salesman for various automobile parts suppliers. None of those jobs paid particularly well. But he also developed a side business taking inventories for the parts departments of assorted GM dealerships.

I was in my early to mid-twenties when his business began to make substantial profits. My younger siblings knew very little about our family's finances during the drinking years. Rather, they expected to eat well, and otherwise live the lifestyle of successful suburbanites.

For my two sisters, both nearly my age, and me this new financial success came as a great surprise. My father, never one to shy away from spending and shunning savings accounts, began to spend wildly, especially on my mother and on the three older children.

On one spendthrift afternoon, my father visited his favorite Chevrolet dealer. He regularly took this company's parts inventory, and was familiar with the owner, parts department employees, and the car salesmen. There, he bought not one, but four new Chevrolets on the same day. My sisters, my mother—she had learned to drive by this time—and I all received brand new Chevrolets as gifts. A lot of cash changed hands that day. Mine was a bright, shiny 1971 Chevrolet convertible. Was this Dad's attempt to make up for all the years of deprivation? I suspect so.

Scene 2: Gun battle in the gully

The bullets were flying left and right. No, this was not a 1950s-era American Wild West television broadcast shown in grainy black and white. This was the real thing! On a bright, but polluted Cleveland summer weekday down in what residents of the neighborhood called the "Ravine," there were three teenage boys wandering the semi-wooded expanse of perhaps 40 or 50 acres of trash dump. I was one of these adventurers.

Near the center of the Ravine was an abandoned railroad tunnel. I am not sure who we found to sell us a box or two of .22 caliber long rifle bullets, but some gullible soul in the neighborhood hardware store sold these live shells to our gang of 14-year-olds. I do not know what the then-current law said about ammunition sales, but I know we acted like we were experienced gunmen.

There were no chain hardware stores in those days so it was to a locally-owned store we went, swaggering in to the first clerk we spotted. "Gimme two boxes of long rifles shells, .22 caliber, please. We have a little hunting to do," one of us blurted.

"Oh, yeah? Do your parents know you're going hunting?" he asked. Lying through our teeth two of us responded almost in unison, "Oh sure. Mom and Dad are regular hunters themselves. Taught us all we know about guns."

What we knew about guns was absolutely nothing. The clerk either believed our story or he simply needed our stash of coins. He walked over to his gun cabinet, and withdrew two boxes of bullets. How proud we were. We had lied and bluffed our way into dozens of real bullets.

How we found the guns in the first place was an easy task. All of our fathers were busy at work, and our mothers seemed to have been pre-occupied with cleaning, cooking, and all those other motherly things. Stevie Warren, a neighbor boy from the next street--by this time, my world had expanded to include all three of the streets on my paper route—had easily procured his father's low-caliber rifle. Bobby Pudzinski, another East 56th Street friend had discreetly smuggled his own father's .22 caliber pistol out of his house in his pocket. No one seemed the wiser about our planned adventure to destroy some glass bottles, and if any desperados should appear, well we would handle them. Now just in case we were ever called into Cuyahoga County's Juvenile Court on gun charges, I had even planned to say something like, "Well, Your Honor, we had a duty to defend ourselves." Ah, the imaginations of the young.

To this day, I do not know how three teenage boys managed to carry a hunting rifle down several streets, including a major thoroughfare, without being stopped by the cops. I can just imagine one of us stuffing a full-sized rifle down the leg on his pants, limping gingerly for ten or twelve city blocks. But, in any case, our walk succeeded without police interference. Perhaps the *local Gestapo* (my father's term, not mine) were all busy at some potential crime scene like Lois Lapka's father's delicatessen on Fleet Avenue at East 55th Street. Here, I will not imply that the police were munching on donuts.

Now that you have all the details, imagine if you will, three teenage boys, guns in hand, standing in front of an old abandoned railroad tunnel nearly in the center of the Ravine. We quickly found some old glass bottles and tin cans, stand-ins for the "bad guys" our imaginations told us were hiding nearby.

Opening fire for about five minutes, we actually hit a few bottles, enjoying the sound of breaking glass. Inexplicably, we were soon startled and confused by pinging sounds coming from directly in front of us. Corresponding to the pings were chunks of dirt jumping up about a foot or so in the air. It took me a few minutes to place the pings and flying bits of dirt, but suddenly my brain clicked—"Bullets, it's bullets!" I shouted. "Someone is shooting at us!"

Smiling and laughing like a boy possessed, I dived into the railroad tunnel which was directly behind us. My friends joined me in our hideout. I had the pistol in hand, and began firing recklessly at... at what, I knew not. I gave no thought whatsoever that we could be shot, wounded, even killed. Or that I might hurt someone else. Oh, adolescence—that time that many of us believe nothing bad could ever happen. Life seemed to go on forever. We were invincible. My high school English teacher often referred to the *existential fact of life* (death is inevitable for all of us) as the "tragic transience of time." This was certainly an opportunity for me to check out of life much earlier than either my parents or I had hoped.

The shooting stopped as quickly as it had started. Our adventure over, I believe we headed to Kozy's Superette, a small ethnic grocery store on the north side of Harvard Avenue between East 58th and East 56th Streets, for a Barq's Root Beer. A good "beer" was always in order after a harrowing gun battle or any other adventure for that matter.

Stevie, Bobby, and I all survived this potential brush with death unscathed. I am not proud of this story—well, OK, I am just a little pleased with my foolishness. My parents never did hear about this adventure. Some things are better left untold to the parental unit.

Scene 3: Loneliness and the goody-two-shoes

In my adolescent years, I sometimes felt lonely. Yet being so quiet and socially awkward complicated my life in at least one way. I wanted to be liked and loved, but my bashfulness prevented me from simply asking for what I needed. Even now, I sometimes enter a room crowded with strangers, and remain for at least a time on the outer edge of an imagined circle. Moving slowly around the perimeter, I look inward for someone I know or someone who looks not only interesting, but nonthreatening. Finally, when I get the nerve to head toward that already-known or interesting, but "safe" person, I take a deep breath, and make a beeline for that person or persons. I am a bit embarrassed by this maneuver of mine in adult years.

To get love or even appreciation as an adolescent, I studied extra hard in school, was scrupulous in my relationship with the Church (that is, in my relationship with God), going to Mass every Sunday, to confession every other Saturday. In short, I acted in whatever ways I thought would get the approval of others, and therefore, acquire their "love." Looking back now, I seem to have been like a chameleon—changing demeanor at will, all in an effort to be liked or loved by the person or group I was with at the time. Of course, I did not know it at the time, but by engaging in this behavior I also failed to present my authentic self, preferring instead to be a goody two shoes, a people-pleaser.

Little Goody Two Shoes is a children's story published by Newbery in 1765. The story made popular the phrase of the same name, and the phrase is used to denote a very virtuous person, a "do-gooder." It is a variation of the Cinderella tale. The story itself tells about the life of Margery Meanwell, a girl who goes through her childhood wearing only one shoe. After a rich man gives her a complete pair of shoes, she becomes ecstatically happy, letting everyone know about her new acquisition. Goody Two Shoes later becomes a teacher, and like Cinderella, marries a wealthy man. Thus, her virtuousness is rewarded with newly-found wealth.

If people "loved" me, it was the "me" I presented to them that they cared for. And that "me" would change depending on the pressure I felt to conform to someone else's view of who I was, and what I stood for. And often the views of others would conflict with one another. My parents, the Church, my neighborhood friends, my classmates at school all seemed to have beliefs that at times were opposed, one with the other.

From various sources I heard that I was smart, shy, quiet, a trouble-maker (with my sisters in my home setting), a sinner who needed to do better, and even an undesirable member of an out-group (here you can alternately insert the words Catholic, Polish, dark-skinned, and so forth). My so-called friends, Brian and Buddy would add still another epithet, "The Chinaman" due to my wintertime sallow skin and the shape of my eyes.

But by the time I reached the age of sixteen, and was a junior in high school, I began to hear the sound of my own voice. And that voice was a humorous one. My first appreciative audience was a fellow high school student, Leroy Stanislaw. One day during a non-work period that is still called "homeroom," I made some silly noise when the room was relatively quiet. It was obvious to most in the classroom who had made the sound. Yet, probably no one was more surprised at the source of the disruptive noise than me and the teacher. This was so out of character for me in a school setting. But, to my great surprise, Leroy laughed right out loud.

"Wow," I thought to myself. "I can be disruptive, and funny, yet there seem to be very few negative consequences." A dirty look from the homeroom monitor was the extent of the price I paid for being a bit of a nuisance to authorities. And, my disruption got me some much-needed attention and perhaps some appreciation from my classmates. I was on my way toward acquiring a reputation as a funny guy, who was not only bright, but deep down, just one of the boys after all. It seems to me now that this change in my behavior was more than establishing a new reputation.

For perhaps the first time in my adolescent, academic years I could show people, other students and teachers alike, that I was worthy of their liking me as a whole person, not just a "brainy" and undersized kid. In some small way, I owe a debt of gratitude to Leroy Stanislaw. He saw a side of me that few others had seen, and his appreciation encouraged me to show more of the person I was becoming.

I saw Leroy Stanislaw one more—this time at a high school reunion. I repeated to him the story about his laughter at my new behavior. Of course, he had no memory of that event. I thanked him anyway for his part in the newer version of "me."

Scene 4: The nun suggests a future

While my parents were enduring their own struggles with alcohol and poverty, I found some support from a surprising source. Looking back on my adolescent years, I realize that there was someone who helped me to decide about my future. In the last month of my senior year in high school, near the end of the spring semester in a civics/government class, a nun cornered me after class one day, inquiring about my future. She asked me a very loaded question filled with her own assumptions, and for which she may have already had a tentative answer. Sister Margaret Thomas said to me, "And you'll be going to college this fall, right?"

I was startled! I could do college level work? Someone believed I could do schooling at that level? I had never once considered getting more education. And now someone seemed to have faith in my academic abilities. This rather large-boned, husky, and outspoken nun had hope for my future, when I had no plans, no sense of direction for my own future. For those keeping score, I was inspired enough by Sr. Margaret Thomas' encouragement to apply for advanced schooling. And I was accepted to the first and only school I had applied to—a private college near my home. That school eventually became a state university by the end of my time there.

Finishing college was not an easy task. I struggled mightily with my studies, especially at the beginning. In fact, my first quarter grades were so low that when I applied for financial aid for the next school year, the financial aid officer laughed at me. "With those grades?" he said, pointing to the paper version of my grade point average (GPA), "You must be kidding!"

I have often thought of returning to that undergraduate school to see that money man. In my fantasy, I would be holding my diploma from the doctoral program I completed in 1993. The title of my dissertation: *The Experience of Having a Broken Heart: A Heuristic Study.*

It's too bad that Sister Margaret Thomas is long since deceased. I would have loved to sit down with her, my hard-covered dissertation copy in hand, and tell her how much her words of support meant to me.

Scene 5: Objects of affection: Rudy Regalado and Ann Rudniski

What story about adolescence would be complete without a little hero worship or some tales of love interests?

As a child and especially as an early adolescent, I had many idols who were baseball players. Their identities changed depending on the kind of season they were having. In general, I was not especially loyal to my idols. If they were having a bad season or even a long stretch of poorly-played games, I would ditch the "player of the hour" like a hot potato.

Some of my heroes' names in the 1950s were: Larry Doby, Al Rosen, Rudy Regalado, Rocky Colavito, and Bob Lemon. What strikes me about this list is that one player, Doby was black and another, Rosen was Jewish. It did not seem to matter to me the ethnic or religious background of the players I idolized. I was color-blind and religion-blind especially when it came to baseball. It seems I was also "Yankee-blind." I had a secret hero who was not all that popular in Cleveland since he was a member of the hated New York Yankees. That player was number seven on the team from the Bronx, Mickey Mantle. It seemed he could hit any pitcher any time he wanted. Lordy, how I envied his bat, his fielding prowess, and his speed afoot.

What I loved about these players is that they were doing exactly what I hoped to do as an adult—play professional baseball. They had made it in the "bigs," and I was a mere hopeful. By the way, Rudy Regalado's full name was Rudolph Valentino Regalado. Apparently Rudy's mother had a fancy for the 1930s movie idol of the same name.

As for romantic (real or imagined) love interests, there was Ann Rudniski. I met Ann while I was with my friend Wally Ostmund. I am not sure how we knew of her existence—perhaps we met her at a movie theater or some other adolescent hangout. In any case, Ann was physically developed beyond her calendar years. That facet of Ann's appearance immediately caught my interest.

She lived far from us on the west side of Cleveland off Scranton Road. It took a long city bus ride on The Cleveland Transit System's Bus Number 18 to visit her, and that we did on several occasions. Sometimes, I went to see her solo, and a few times Wally went with me. I suppose what I liked about Ann was that she seemed to like *me*. It was gratifying that someone of the opposite sex thought I was worth talking to and hanging out with. I saw her off and on, mostly off, for about a year, then I lost interest and I never saw her again. I sometimes wonder how her life turned out.

I fondly remember Ann and I believe that her presence in my life was a precursor to my later serious dating. Thinking of Ann now, I regard her as a sort of boot camp instructor. She taught me that I had something to offer the opposite sex. Relating to her served as training for my later heterosexual relationships. Many thanks to you, Ann!

My friend Wally was not so fortunate with women or with life in general. Less than ten years after our adventures with Ann, I would hear that Wally had died in Vietnam, the victim of a sniper's bullet. Wally always was a risk-taker. Even the fact that it was the United States Marine Corps he chose to join during the Vietnam era provided him with an opportunity for adventure and danger. It seems the Marines are often among the first to be sent into precarious and dangerous situations.

Although he and I drifted apart once I moved to another part of Cleveland from the Harvard Avenue neighborhood, I still miss my friend to this day. Readers who might like to get in "touch" with Wally can travel to Washington, DC. His name and those of thousands of his deceased colleagues are etched into the wall of the Vietnam Veterans Memorial Wall. The wall itself consists of two black granite slabs that measure 246 feet, 9 inches. It seems that Wally and I have found very different ways to achieve early earthly immortality—me with my memoir and he with his place secured in America's capital.

Visiting the Vietnam Veterans Memorial Wall on several

occasions, I can't help but get teary-eyed at Wally's demise. Like many of my childhood friends, he led a difficult life. And his death was anything but pleasant. To die from a bullet wound in a jungle nearly 9000 miles from home and among mere acquaintances, and enemy combatants would not be the way I would chose to go.

Maybe it does not matter the circumstances of our inevitable end. But I hope my demise mimics my father's—reclining in a room filled those who loved me in life, and who cared enough to stay with me, ushering me out the door.

ACT THREE
Early Adulthood

Scene 1: Mackerel-snappers make the best Marines

I thought I was like everyone else, and then Karen Krandahl (not her real name) made her comments about Catholics. At the luncheon table with five or six other freshmen college students present, she said "I don't mind Catholics, I just don't understand them." I took her words as a put-down, and a statement of her superior status as a _____ (I never did ask Karen what her religious preference was). At the time of this event, I was a mere 18 years old.

As I was eating my fish sandwich on that Friday during Lent, her comments on Catholics was how Karen started the conversation. I was so shocked that I did not make any reply initially. Although she did not specifically call me that 1950s-era religious slur, *mackerel snapper*, Karen seemed to have a little something in common with the actor, Robert Mitchum. In the 1944 film, *Heaven Knows, Mr. Allison*, U. S. Marine corporal Allison (Mitchum) refers to Catholics as mackerel snappers while he is speaking to a Catholic nun. Trying to soften his *faux pas*, Allison explains that some of the finest Marines are Catholic.

For those not familiar with Catholic tradition, until recently Catholics beginning at age 14 were required to abstain from eating meat every Friday of the year. Instead, they could substitute fish. This rule was peculiar to Catholics and distinguished them from other Christians. This stricture has been lessened in the late twentieth century. Now, Catholics age 14 and older need to abstain from eating meat only on Ash Wednesday, Good Friday, and on all Fridays during Lent. Catholics ages 18 to 59 are currently required to fast during Lent, a tradition that says they can eat only one full meal on

Fridays, except if their health requires a larger food intake.

Growing up I lived in a neighborhood that was almost entirely Catholic—it was situated at the intersection of two ethnic neighborhoods *Warszawa* and *Krakowa*. Although these two "villages" were nominally Polish or housed those of Polish descent, there were other varieties of Catholics from other backgrounds. For example, one of my good friends in the neighborhood was a Czech Catholic, while another was a Welsh Catholic.

I suppose that when I was eighteen, I naively thought that everyone was either a Catholic or at least, tolerated us. One of my personal missions since the mid-1970s has been to become the family story teller and recorder of tales. In a sense then, I felt relieved to find so many Protestants on my grandmother Mary Underwood's side of the family. One particular Protestant, the Reverend Doctor Rowland Taylor, is considered a saint in several Protestant churches. More about Dr. Taylor's life follows below.

Should I ever see Karen Krandahl again, I could flash my Protestant family tree at her. "Five hundred years of family history without a single Catholic on one particular line of my family. See that Karen, I belong after all." I never did tell Karen I was a practicing Catholic. And even now I am a bit ashamed of my lack of courage and of my great desire to be liked and accepted even if it meant not revealing my true self to those whose approval I seemed to want.

Perhaps the most well-known of these Protestant ancestors was the Reverend Rowland Taylor (1510-1555). Just days after Queen Mary's accession to the throne of England, she ordered Rowland Taylor arrested, and brought before Bishop Stephen Gardiner for examination. Although Taylor was questioned thoroughly by Bishop Gardiner, he was soon released. Apparently, "Bloody Mary," as she became known, was not ready to issue her final judgments and their accompanying punishments this early in her reign.

Essentially, Rowland Taylor was a "victim" of his time in history. He was born in 1510 during the reign of King Henry VIII (1491-1547). Henry was nicknamed "Defender of the Faith" for his many defenses of Catholic beliefs. Yet, he was also a monarch who so wanted a male heir to his throne, that he was willing to defy the Pope in Rome. Henry first married Catherine of Aragon. Catherine gave him only a female child (Mary), and as time passed Henry was convinced there was no hope for gaining a male child and heir through Catherine. Thus, began a battle between Canterbury, London, and Rome that would last for decades. The final act in the battle over beliefs would be a complete and very painful separation between the faithful of England and those of Rome. Rowland would pay for this separation with his very life.

On July 25, 1553, Rowland Taylor was arrested for the first time. He was tentatively charged with heresy for preaching falsehoods at Bury St. Edmunds. He had been appointed Archdeacon at this parish a few years earlier (1548) with much fanfare. In his sermon, Taylor had denounced the Catholic practice of priestly celibacy. After a period of questioning about his beliefs, Taylor was released and he continued his ministry. This was only the beginning of his troubles with Queen Mary I.

On January 22, 1555 Rowland Taylor, John Hooper, William Barlow, and Edward Crome were all arrested and brought before Bishop Gardiner for trial. While Crome recanted, Hooper, Barlow, and Taylor did not. In fact, Taylor was particularly obstinate and even aggressive in his statements. He accused Gardiner of violating the oaths of allegiance he had taken before Henry VIII and Edward VI. It was a standoff, but Gardiner held the upper hand as he was not only a bishop, but was the Lord Chancellor of England. Taylor was excommunicated from the Catholic Church and symbolically stripped of his ministerial garments.

Taylor was given one final opportunity to reject his "heretical" beliefs. On January 29, 1555, Taylor again appeared before Gardiner and was asked to recant. Instead, he restated his Protestant beliefs in no uncertain terms, and as a result the Reverend Dr. Rowland Taylor was sentenced to die at the stake. He was also offered a final meal with his family.

Taken back to his home town of Hadleigh, Taylor met with his wife at St. Mary's Church. The two spoke only briefly, then he was handed over to the Sheriff of Essex at Chelmsford. Rowland was to become only the third person put to death on orders from Queen Mary I. Rogers had been executed on February 4 and Saunders on February 8.

On February 9, 1555, Taylor was taken to Aldham Common, just outside Hadleigh, England. A local butcher was ordered to light the pyre that surrounded Taylor, but he refused. Several onlookers then threw lighted torches on the wood pile. But before the flames could consume Taylor, a "friendly" guard hit Taylor on the head with his halberd, probably killing him instantly. A halberd was a two-handed weapon about five or six feet long. It was used quite often in the 14th and fifteenth century battles.

Still, when I discovered dozens of well-known Catholic ancestors on my maternal grandfather's side of the family tree, I could quietly rejoice. Mom and Dad would have been proud had they known of these ancestors, Catholic and Protestant alike. Just briefly, among those saintly Catholic ancestors were Sts. Chlotilde of Burgundy (475-548 AD/CE), Itta/Itte (592-652 AD/CE), Bertha (c. 539/565-612 AD/CE), Sigrada/Sigrade of Verdun (605-678 AD/CE), Begga of Landen (615-693), and Margaret of Scotland (1045-1093 (AD/CE).

I like to think that if I met Karen again, I would remind her of our earlier encounter, and disclose my religious beliefs to her. And with a note of pride in my voice, I can imagine revealing to her my list of a single Protestant saint in my family tree, and the half dozen or so of the Catholic variety. On the other hand, perhaps I am now sure enough of my identity that I could ignore Karen's comments from the 1960s, and simply rejoice in renewing an old acquaintance.

Scene 2: Sink or swim: Stormy times ahead

Let's face it—When I was nineteen-years-old, I was a young adult in chronological age only. Emotionally, I was probably about age 15 when my college offered me a chance to go to Washington, DC to take a cooperative education job with the *Washington Post* newspaper. Cooperative education provides a student with "real life work experience", while he/she officially continues to be a full time student.

In truth though, there was no formal job interview, no resume submitted, and little or no chance that a student would be turned down for a particular job. I even had a choice between working for the *St. Louis Post-Dispatch* or for the venerable and politically liberal *Post* in Washington. As a budding young history major and English minor, it was an easy decision for me to go to the heart of American politics, the District of Columbia.

On one fine autumn day five decades ago, I packed up my two-tone, black and white, 1956 Chevrolet four-door model 210, and hit the road ready for the action in the nation's capital. I even had a place to stay in the *District*, since one of my school's other cooperative education students already had a residence there. In an earlier telephone conversation, Joe (not his real name) had invited me to stay with him and three other housemates.

With hindsight, moving into that 150-year-old dump of a residence (and I am using that term not pejoratively, but as a liberally kind description) was probably a mistake. The house was badly in need of repair, as were many of the homes in the inner city of Washington. Still, I was happy to have a place to lay my head at night. My comfort there was soon to be interrupted on a Saturday morning.

College students often go out drinking on Friday nights. In fact, studies conducted by the Centers for Disease Control have shown that about one in six adults in the United States engage in binge drinking about four times each month. The average amount of alcohol ingested per binge is eight drinks. Although such high alcohol intake is reported across the lifespan, it is most common in younger adults aged 18-34. https://www.cdc.gov/alcohol/facts-sheets/binge-drinking.htm Retrieved 2/5/2018.

I believe my housemates helped to pad those binge-drinking numbers that Friday night. Waking early on that fateful Saturday—my housemates still fast asleep--I entered the kitchen intending to make a hearty breakfast for myself.

Suddenly, I halted in disbelief. Apparently, my housemates had had the "munchies" after their night of debauchery. They had left a very large frying pan on the stove and it was loaded with what appeared to be bacon grease. Perched on the edge of the pan were three or four very large rats that were too busy lapping up the grease to notice my entry into the room. Or perhaps they had dealt with people like me before, and simply had no fear of my presence. Ignoring me, these critters kept on lapping up their own version of breakfast. After a few seconds of confusion at what I was seeing, I confirmed the genus and species of my unexpected fellow diners. Not wanting to turn my posterior to these critters, I backed carefully out of that room, leaving breakfast to the non-human and uninvited house guests. I soon found other housing accommodations.

Seeing these creatures put me in mind of the rats that inhabited the backyard of my East 57th Street home in Cleveland's inner city. There, I had lived in fear of my parents telling me to take out the trash. Doing so meant an encounter with a group of slightly smaller species of Cleveland-based rats. I never did tell my parents why I resisted doing this seemingly easy chore of taking garbage out to the trash cans in the rear of the yard. I did not like living with rats then, and my attitude toward these creatures has not changed with time's passing.

As it turned out, rats were the least of my Washington worries. The job itself provided with me with other opportunities—both positive and negative. The positive included working with some of the best journalists, photographers, and cartoonists in the newspaper business. Bill Brady, the sports editor, and Herb Block, the nationally-renowned cartoonist, were just two of the staff who treated me and the other low-ranking employees with great respect. I am grateful to them for that. Additionally, the autumn I spent in DC was the tail-end of a presidential election year. I met several politicians who I would never have had the chance to see in most other venues. Hubert Humphrey and the daughter of Lyndon Johnson, Linda Bird, were but two of these characters.

My duties at the *Post* included taking newspaper copy from one area of the newsroom to the reporters and editors who were seated elsewhere in the newsroom. I was also required to enter the wire room—a large area where the *Post* kept its cumbersome and ever-busy machines that cranked out stories and reports from wire services such as Reuters, the Associated Press, and United Press International.

Gathering these printed wire stories off the machines gave me an opportunity to take a gander at the bulletin board that was mounted on the wall outside the wire room. On that bulletin board were listings of various items for sale, housing for rent or sale, and personal notices of one kind or another. One particular advertisement caught my adventure-seeking attention. Someone had placed a notice that said something like "Experienced sailors needed to shepherd the sloop *SS Constitution* (here I am exaggerating a bit) from its current berth in Atlantic City, New Jersey to its home port in Annapolis, Maryland."

Being an experienced sailor—I had once paddled a row boat in the fresh-water La Due Reservoir in Chagrin Falls, Ohio—I soon telephoned the advertiser offering my services. To my surprise, he readily accepted my offer. In the near future, I would be disappointing that owner/advertiser to no end.

The ship's owner who also served as its captain, I, and three others all piled into the owner's nearly-new, dark gray Chrysler van and headed off to Atlantic City. We arrived at that city's harbor at about ten p.m. for what would be a memorable and dangerous trip. For an hour or so, we did all the things that sailors do before a voyage. Since I had never even seen the ocean before or been anywhere closer to a sailboat than ten miles away, I have no memory of what all needed to be done pre-voyage. In truth, I had no idea what I was doing on a 30-foot sloop on that fateful Friday evening in late October.

We finally set sail about midnight bound for Annapolis, home of the United States Naval Academy. Atlantic City's harbor was relatively calm, a condition I assumed the rest of the voyage would be like. I was wrong. I was so inexperienced with boats, ships, and other water craft that I did not know that harbors were chosen for their sites mainly due to their depth and the shelter they provided from the weather.

Almost as soon as we entered open water, the seas began to churn. None of the "hired" help--we all worked only for the thrill of the adventure--had bothered to check the weather forecast at the outset of our journey. I am not sure the captain/owner did either. And if he did bother, I suspect that he realized that winter was fast approaching, and this particular weekend might be his last chance to return his ship to its home port before the weather turned even worse.

It seems that we left Atlantic City just after an autumn storm had hit the east coast. We definitely found the remnants of that troublesome weather. The wind began to blow at an estimated forty miles per hour, and the waves hit the ship at a height I guessed to be twenty to thirty feet. Mind you now, I am no judge of anything marine-related, but in my amateurish opinion, the weather had turned very bad. In other words, we were now in for the ride of my short (up to this point) life.

At first I handled the wind and waves well for an aquatic tenderfoot. Nearly three hours out of port, I started to feel a headache coming on. Later in my life I would learn that my personal version of seasickness was always preceded by a headache. And seasick I did get.

Initially, I simply went below deck hoping that if I did not actually see how stormy it was, I would gain my sea legs, or whatever it is that real sailors say. Again, I was wrong. The longer I stayed below deck, the worse I felt. My headache was now being accompanied by nausea. So topside I went, again hoping to defeat my symptoms.

Not wishing to scandalize my dear readers, let me just say that at first I attempted to discreetly lean over the edge of the ship (or whatever that edge is called in ship-speak) to relieve my stomach of its contents. That attempt lasted about ten minutes. Soon, I lost all dignity and merely crawled along the deck allowing my now-defenseless body to do its own natural thing. I was officially out of control of my bodily functions.

Surprisingly, I felt no shame in displaying my motion-generated illness. What I did worry about was how the captain would respond to my behavior. After all, I had hinted to him that I was an old sea-hand, and that I could handle the relatively short trip from Atlantic City to Annapolis.

Making a long and tortuous story shorter, let me say here that I survived the trip. And so did the captain and my fellow shipmates. But we never did make it to Annapolis. The weather proved too difficult to navigate the full length of our itinerary. Instead, we merrily turned southwestward to Cape May, still in the state of New Jersey. Entering Cape May's harbor, the seas again turned relatively gentle.

Once we docked at a pier, all of us hustled to that board-thingy that goes onto the dock—I believe the board is officially called the "gangway." I had hoped to escape this embarrassing ordeal without seeing the captain for fear I would hear a lecture and some encouragement to never respond again to any bulletin board notices. To my pleasant surprise, the captain was amazingly conciliatory. He inquired as to my health this fine sunny morning, and wished me well on my work at the newspaper. I said good-bye to him rather sheepishly, and walked a few blocks to the Greyhound bus station. I had just enough money to return to Washington for my next shift at the newspaper.

While I am not proud of this misadventure, I am pleased to report that that was the last time I ever became seasick. Since this 1960s-era ocean voyage, I have visited the islands of St. Thomas, St. Croix, Puerto Rico, St. Kitts, and a handful of island ports in South and Central America by ship, all without a single bout of illness. Of course, this report on my health does not include the respiratory infection I contracted on St. Thomas a few years ago. Please note that I do not feel any embarrassment about that recent bout with island illness. And this time, there was no sea captain to whom I could make excuses.

Several years earlier, I had received a notice from the U.S. government to report to my local draft office for a pre-induction physical. This was in the Vietnam War period of the late 1960's and early 1970's. Many of my contemporaries were quickly joining the Navy or Coast Guard in order to avoid being drafted into the infantry of the United States Army. I felt no such urgency to avoid ground-based military duty in Vietnam. Even that sounded better to me than spending time aboard an ocean-going ship with any of the maritime branches of service. I had learned my lesson well!

For the record, I was never drafted into the U.S. Army's infantry. Perhaps, my draft board had received word about my misadventures on the Atlantic, deciding I would have made a questionable soldier as well.

Scene 3: Meeting Karla at the Quarries

Dating and I were relative strangers to each other. By the time I was 21 years old, I may have had as many as ten real dates. Oh, in high school I went with a group of friends, both male and female, to football games and to other school-related events, but I don't consider those to be authentic two-person dates. My innate bashfulness rendered me without serious female company until I was in my early twenties.

That all changed one fine June morning at a county-owned swimming hole which was located within a public park called *The Berea Quarries*. I came to the park by myself, ostensibly to study for some college history class or other. And I did study for an hour or so. But all the while, I was aware of a pretty young woman lying on a blanket near mine. She was sitting with two other women, but this particular young person was situated on the part of their blanket closest to me. I sometimes have wondered what would have happened if this specific person of interest had been on the other end of their shared space. Would I have spoken to them, and then eventually dated one of her colleagues present at the park that day instead of my nearest blanket neighbor?

My first words to this young woman, whom I later learned was called Karla, show just how inexperienced I was with the dating/mating game. Looking at Karla intently, I lightly said, "What do you do for an encore?" She had been singing along to some '60s-era rock and roll song playing on her radio. I have since discovered that adolescents and young adults do not do much of anything without "my music" blaring in the background.

Surprised, I would imagine, at the cleverness of my question, Karla muttered back to me, "Oh, well, ah, let's see now.... ." I could see right then, that this was going to be a serious relationship. No, not really. As it turned out, she was already dating some guy named Danny, a fellow student she had met at her suburban high school. Although she gave me her telephone number—I suspect she enjoyed the chase—she was quick to let me know she already had a beau.

We even exchanged letters with each other via the United States Postal Service with me telling her how interested in her I was. She sometimes responded by saying rather dramatically I might add, that "You are disturbing my quietude." Is *quietude* an authentic English word or was that something she heard on some quintessential television soap opera such as, *As the World Turns*? Still, I must have done or said something right over the coming months because she eventually ditched her high school love. Thus began my first really serious romantic relationship.

As for our dating encounters, I don't recall those times being especially significant. We went to movies, parks, and entertainment events like baseball games (yes, she was a baseball fan). And we watched a lot of television in the basement of her parents' home.

I also recall feeling uncomfortable in her parents' presence. Karla's mother seldom smiled around me. I remember thinking that much of the time she seemed angry, irritated, or just plain upset, especially with her husband. To be fair, I knew very little about her childhood or about her marriage to Karla's father. Perhaps, she had good reason to be angry or upset.

Her father was often not at home when I visited Karla at her house. He owned a bar that was located across from a 1940s-style dance hall in the inner city of Cleveland. The bar was often busy immediately before or shorty after a dance at the club. Mr. Jones (not his real name) held a jeweler's license and he dealt in the sale of diamonds and other fine jewels during the lulls between his deliveries of drinks to his patrons at the bar.

I hesitate to speak ill of the late Mr. Jones, but I sometimes wondered if there were some shady goings-on in his acquisitions and sales of precious stones. I am not sure why I suspected that, but his friendships with Cleveland policemen and his many whispered conversations with them at the bar may have been a factor in my suspicions. He also dealt in the sale of airline tickets. In those days, tickets could be readily and legally transferred from one person to another. The origins of these tickets were also a mystery to me, and I could get no clear answers about them when I inquired. Again, he operated this side business out of the bar.

Karla's father also carried "heat" with him wherever he went. His gun was a small, ivory-handled .22-caliber revolver. As if that were not protection enough, he regularly carried with him a pair of what he called *brass knucks*. For the uninformed, knucks are a "self-defense solution of the highest quality," according to today's number one seller of such devices, Knockout Knucks. Brass knuckles are designed to slip over the tips of the fingers, nestling at the mid-point of the back of the hand. They are manufactured in such a way as to inflict maximum damage on the face of the unlucky person on the receiving end of a punch. I suppose it was little wonder I felt uncomfortable around Karla's mother and father.

Karla and I dated for about a year and a half before the story gets sticky for me. Being a naïve and emotionally young Catholic, I believed what I had been taught years earlier--that there was to be no sex before marriage. I had added my own addendum to that dictum. And that was if you did have sex before marriage, it had better be with someone you intended to marry. Hearing that statement now, I am feeling rather naïve.

Good grief, I think my face is turning red with embarrassment, half a lifetime later. I sometimes wonder if my marriage was doomed from the beginning. Might I have married with too little relationship experience? Might she have been too young at the time of our marriage when she had not yet reached age 21? With my belief system, the fact that I felt almost forced to marry someone because I had sex with her certainly put me/us at a disadvantage. Although she was also a Catholic, I am not sure why she agreed to the marriage. I believe she may already have been sexually experienced (is that unchivalrous of me to suggest this possibility?). Might she have actually loved me and intended to stay with me for the balance of our lives? I may never know the answers to these questions.

Nearly sixteen years later and after the births of two beautiful children following our marriage in a Catholic church in a western suburb of Cleveland, the marriage ended. In the decades that followed, I often thought, "If only I had not married her I would have saved myself much pain." Yet, I would not have experienced things like living in the Virgin Islands, taking that exotic family trip to Mexico, buying that beautiful '68 Camaro, or being involved in the

Marriage Encounter movement. Most importantly, I would not have "met" and loved my children, Sean and Nicole. How sad I still feel today thinking about how much of my children's lives I missed by getting divorced. Our children were 12 and 9 years old at the time of the breakup.

Having joint legal and physical custody of the children created its own problems. Karla and I seldom communicated about the children or about anything else for that matter. I felt in great pain in general, and my aches only increased when I spoke to her. For her part, Karla told me that the way she got by following our divorce was to pretend that I was dead. I suppose I may have cooperated with her wishes by generally feeling as if I were deceased. Feeling dead while one is still is alive is unpleasant to say the least.

There is no easy way to be divorced when children are involved in a split-up. But more about this major loss in Act Four, Scene 1.

Scene 4: Marriage & the domestic Peace Corps

In spite of my early struggles with my college studies, I did graduate from the University (when I started the school had been a mere "college") in the late 1960s. In fact, I married only a few weeks before my June graduation. I was twenty-three years old. Although I was a novice at being a college graduate and a newlywed, I began to experience some additional important times in my life. The more significant events surrounding this period of my life might even be called milestones. They were certainly pivotal in my search for an identity and for helping me to notice that my values were changing.

One of the most significant of these milestones was moving to the Virgin Islands. Karla and I had just joined the Volunteers in Service to America (VISTA), a program designed by Lyndon Johnson, probably as a sequel to the Peace Corps movement established by President John Kennedy.

At the time we were both in our early twenties and had been married for only three weeks. We and fifteen other couples were recruited to run preschools in the Caribbean. Even though the schools were intended to help young children who were legal citizens of the Virgin Islands, the truth is, the poorer sections of the VI were populated by non-citizen immigrants from the British, French, Dutch, and Spanish islands of the Caribbean.

It was a hot, humid day in late June when we arrived on the island of St. Croix. There were no covered jet-ways in those days, so when we deplaned, it was into the late afternoon of a Caribbean summer day. The sun was exceptionally hot, and the air felt like it was loaded to capacity with dampness. This was not the ideal introduction to a very different life than I had known while growing up in America. My first thought after traveling all day—there were no direct flights to the island then—was to turn around, asking the pilot to fly me back to Cleveland. Much to my surprise, I did not ask.

The building that the program officials drove us to was a former Danish orphanage that was built about 1820. This was to be our home for the next six weeks as we trained to serve the people of these former Danish islands. What I did not know at the time was that my wife and I had been selected to share a bedroom with another married couple. I never knew why nor did I ask about the rationale for choosing us to share such an intimate space. If this housing arrangement seems uncomfortable, please note that it was at best, inconvenient.

Old Queen Louise Home, St. Croix, Virgin Islands

The bedroom was small and our half of the boudoir was separated from the other only by a short screen. Good grief--still another reason to head back home to the mainland!

I believe the dinner on that first night was designed to immerse us in the culture of the typical poor household of the Caribbean. On our plates that night was *fungi*, a dish of pineapple-laced *okra* that was obviously overcooked, *breadfruit*, a starchy vegetable only slightly reminiscent of potatoes, and a very unique main course of *roast goat*. I ate only the chunks of pineapple, going to bed hungry. I slept little that night, how could I with our roommates snoring so loudly?

The next morning I awakened to the sound of a rooster crowing nearby. To say, as Southerners do, that I felt *cattywampus* would be an understatement. Both my mind and my body were askew and I felt bewildered. Soon I realized it was six a.m. but already light. Once again, I longed to go home not just soon, but immediately. Yet although I complained mightily, I did not resign from this assignment.

Instead, I simply covered my head with a pillow, hoping to get some much-needed additional sleep. But hearing our noisy roommates, I knew I was awake for the day. Wondering what was for breakfast this fine day—I would actually have enjoyed a dish of baked rooster—I waited for my turn in the shared bathroom.

Training began that first full day after our initial evening meal. Our instruction consisted of six long weeks of learning to teach pre-school children who were from a culture other than our own, and discovering how to run a school. The training was helpful in that I learned some things about how to increase children's learning. In undergraduate school, I had been schooled to memorize historical events in the history classes I took, not how to teach young children.

Six weeks to the day of our arrival in St. Croix, we were given our permanent assignments. The Virgin Islands' assignments were to spread out among three islands—St. Croix, St. John, and St. Thomas. We had expressed a desire to be sent to St. Thomas to live among the French-speaking people of a section of that island known as *Frenchtown*. Frenchtown was a small fishing village occupied mostly by émigrés from the French island of Saint-Barthelemy (AKA St. Bart's).

There were also a small number of people in that village who had emigrated from some of the British islands such as Nevis, St. Kitts, Anguilla, and Antigua. This British group was among the very poorest on the island. Touring the outer edges of Frenchtown, I was shocked to see two or three families living in a single shack made of corrugated steel and cardboard, and without proper sanitation or running water. This was what I came to the Caribbean to help change.

Making a very long story much shorter, we soon began to recruit children to attend our school. We still did not have a building for our proposed school, but we had our eye on a brand new one owned by Altagracia Wenner.

Mrs. Wenner was all too happy to have the United States Government pay her a rather outrageous rental fee every month. For our part, we not only taught school on the second floor of her building, we lived on that same floor in very simple surroundings.

The school seems to have been a success. The children loved coming to learn, and we learned to love our charges. They were all in all, very sweet five and six-year-olds. Of the 10 or twelve children who came to us to learn how to color, paste, and sing songs, only one, Mark Lacroix, was actually French. I do not know if the nationalities of the other children or the color of their skin kept other French children away from our lessons, or if they simply could afford schooling elsewhere. I do know that my knowledge of the French language did me little good in my work.

An exception to my lack of opportunities to speak French came during Sunday Mass at St. Anne's, the little Catholic Church that sat at the top of the hill in Frenchtown.

I am surprised to have remembered the name of that little church on the hill in Frenchtown, but I will never forget the older French women who came to Mass dressed in their finest clothes, which were always entirely black. I could imagine them all living on an eighteenth century sugar plantation back in St. Barthelemy or on some other French Caribbean island hundreds of years earlier, all dressed exactly as they now were, wearing very conservative and very black dresses, shoes, scarves, and stockings. I think the elderly women of the island were impressed that I could speak their language, although my accent may have thrown them off a bit. Their own French was a patois, not dissimilar to the patois English spoken by those island residents whose mother tongue was a unique and lyrical version of English.

In spite of the success of our school, the time we spent in the Caribbean was very difficult. It seemed hot and very humid every day, and we rejoiced when on the very coldest day of winter, and in the middle of the night, the temperature plummeted to 69 degrees Fahrenheit! There were no real movie theaters, no plays to attend, no bowling alleys, no affordable restaurants except those that served my least favorite dish, roast goat. Still, I might have been willing to eat roast rooster had it been offered to me.

Yet, overall, I gained much during this experience. Perhaps the most significant lesson I learned was that I could survive trying experiences. I could tolerate very harsh conditions, those that were a million miles away from what I had grown up with. Of the 16 couples who trained with us, only ten couples stayed the course. Only twenty people out of the original 32 continued to live in difficult situations on Caribbean islands that were on average only twelve miles long and four miles wide. None of the volunteers had a car much less a boat. Nor did my wife and I have much money. The U.S. government paid us the paltry sum of fifty dollars per month. Still, the Federal government paid our rent, gave us an allowance for food, and covered our insurance expenses, and even saved seventy-five dollars per month for us in a bank account on the mainland. But, for disposable income, we had only what we were paid monthly plus anything we could beg from mainland relatives, which in my case was not much.

Then, there were the cultural differences. Our neighbor, a butcher by trade, and a native of St. Barth's, became disenchanted with our island-born dog, Antilles. Certainly, he was not interested in the fact that the dog might have been important to one of his neighbors. As a butcher, he may also have not given much value to animal life. After all, he spent many hours each day carving up the bodies of cows, pigs, and other critters. While looking out our side window one hot summer day, during our second year in the Virgin Islands, I heard a frightful howl, as if some animal were being butchered. In fact, it was our pet who now stumbled back to our house with a large butcher knife stuck in her back. Apparently, she came too close for the butcher's comfort.

After carrying our dog Antilles back to our building, I carefully removed the knife from her back. Somehow the knife missed her vital organs, and while she continued to howl, she was very much alive. I wrapped a towel around her. Put her in the government car we were fortunate to have had loaned to us for that particular day, and I drove her to the nearest veterinarian's office. The vet was appalled when I told him the story. Making a long and painful story shorter, Antilles recovered from her wounds. The vet was so incensed with the attacker that he charged us nothing for his services, if we promised to take the butcher to court.

We did just that. I have no specific memory of what transpired at court during the trial of the "Butcher of Charlotte Amalie, Virgin Islands," as I now like to call him. But for whatever the reason, he was declared not guilty (by reason of insanity?). We then spent the rest of our time in St. Thomas seeing the butcher glare at us with what seemed to be a small smirk on his face. We left the island, returning to the United States the next month as our term of service had expired, with a now-recovered Antilles in tow. It was just as well that we chose to not extend our service to VISTA. I don't believe I could have continued to face this man without harsh words being exchanged.

I am proud that we were able to endure the entire time of our service. Granted, other couples were even more isolated than we were. Loneliness and homesickness can be awful maladies. I believe that the ability to persevere, to tolerate troubling circumstances, is vital to discovering family histories and chronicling family tales. Such an ability to persevere, despite hours of frustrating research that often produces nothing useful, is an invaluable trait for those who keep track of the family history.

In spite of what I thought was often a tortuous way of life, I stayed in that very foreign environment. Missing my family of origin greatly, I recall pining to return to the United States' mainland, and to reunite with my parents and my seven siblings.

Still, I met fascinating people in these Caribbean islands—people whose cultures were dramatically different from my own. To some degree, the French people of our village accepted me, almost as one of their own! The children in our school and their parents apparently cherished our presence and seemed to be saddened by our departure. Perhaps they all learned at least a little something from us. We certainly learned from them.

Further, through my experiences in the Caribbean, I learned to persist, to continue toward some distant goal, even when I was confronted by great odds. I believe this ability to stay the course has helped me to become a better researcher of family stories and perhaps even become a more effective storyteller. As a writer, I know I also gathered rich material and some tales to share with my family, friends, and others when I returned to the United States. All in all, the time I spent living on a small island was good practice for a budding family history writer.

Scene 5: Love letters and a reason for living

While my life in the Caribbean may sound like some idyllic adventure (especially on frigid winter days), life has way of turning things around in the blink of an eye. My marriage had survived more than a year of *sturm und drang* under very difficult circumstances in the Caribbean, but it would not survive more than the next decade and a half in the United States. We had been married for five or six years when Karla and I began to serve as group leaders for a Catholic Church movement called *Marriage Encounter*.

This undertaking began in Spain in 1952 as a series of conferences for married couples. Its founder was a young Spanish priest, Father Gabriel Calvo. Calvo's goal was to encourage couples to develop an open and honest relationship within their marriage, while living out a sacramental way of being in service to others. By the late 1960s, the Marriage Encounter movement had spread to the United States under the leadership of Father Chuck Gallagher. And by the twenty-first century, the ME movement as it came to be known can be experienced by couples, Catholic, Protestant, and Jewish alike, in dozens of countries across the globe.

In Marriage Encounter, couples learned to communicate openly through a process of writing to each other daily. The letters were intended to "clear the air" between the individuals, thus completing much of the unfinished business that people often leave unsaid, and therefore, unresolved. I am not sure how many of the lead couples ended up divorced, but we certainly became one of them. While the seeds of the breakup may have been sown during the time in the Caribbean, it did not reach its climax until I reached middle age, that is my late thirties.

I still have many of the notebooks that Karla and I used to

exchange "love letters" during the three or four years we were involved in Marriage Encounter. I am not sure why I would keep such mementos from that earlier era. Perhaps, I am simply a romantic, hesitant to let go of a happy time from my past. Or as a budding writer, I may see these letters as fodder for some future book about marriage.

Some of these letters are especially intense. For example, on the Sunday of the two-day Marriage Encounter weekend, couples are asked to separately write answers, and I do mean write for the entire allotted two hours on this question: *"Why do I want to go living?"* Even now, I find myself taking a deep breath and a mighty gulp on imagining my answer to this question. Prior to leaving the room, the couple is then told that if they should run out of "material" to write about, they should answer a second question, *"Why do I want to go on living with you?"* Believe me, these two questions are the fodder for many, many tears. Honestly though, I feel most alive when I experience deep, but difficult emotions such as those I felt in Marriage Encounter. Perhaps this is why I have saved these ME notebooks—to remind myself that life is truly worth living.

Scene 6: I could teach what and where?

I was once asked to write about something that happened in my life that changed the way I thought or behaved. Upon reflection, I suppose that getting my first college teaching job changed the way I thought about myself and changed the way I behaved. At the age of 25, I earned a masters' degree from the University of Pittsburgh. My first mother-in-law, who was generally not very nice to me, said at my graduation, "You'll be teaching college now, won't you?"

Her words were all I needed to send my thinking in a new direction. Me, teach college? How could I teach such students? Did I have anything to offer them? Maybe I did, maybe not. At least I could try to do such work. I began sending letters of application and a resume to a few post-secondary schools near my home in Summit County, Ohio.

Amazingly, some responded to me. And one college in the Akron/Cleveland area asked me in for an interview. Before I left the interview that day, I had in my hand an offer to teach. When they offered me the phenomenal salary of *$8000 per year*, I did not hesitate—I accepted the offer on the spot.

In some ways, this event reminded me of my experience with Sister Margaret Thomas in my senior year of high school. She had confidence in me—she thought I could go to college. Now, my newly-found supervisor expressed his faith in my abilities. If you are beginning to see a pattern here, you are right. I seemed to need at least one other person to tell me I could _____ (feel free to fill in the blank here). I know that confidence is supposed to come from within, but in those days (and perhaps still), I needed outside support and encouragement to make important decisions.

My euphoria over the new position did not last long. In the

summer of the year that I was to start teaching full-time, my department chair asked me to go down to a high school in Canton, Ohio to teach a single class. My students were to be a large group of full time K through 12 teachers who needed to take a continuing education class. They were all at least twenty years *older* than I was. I was soon trembling with fear. What if these experienced educators found out I had no idea what I was talking about or that I was an inexperienced teacher who displayed no effective teaching methods?

Miracles do happen! I managed to get through this summer course, and no one laughed at me. In fact, their reviews of my performance were good. They thought I did a fine job, and some even said they learned some important things. I determined right then to continue teaching as a career. This was a good idea, since I had already signed a teaching contract for the next school year.

From this point on, I begin to change the way I thought of myself. I was a real teacher now, a college teacher at that! And some students thought I had something useful to say that would enhance their knowledge. Wow! I could hardly believe my good fortune! I was still frightened about the quality of my abilities, but I found that I was actually excited now to begin a new career.

The shy little kid from the inner city of Cleveland was beginning to create a new way of seeing himself and a new way of behaving. It would be a long haul to change my way of thinking about my world. What is that Chinese proverb—the journey of a thousand miles begins with a single step? Let the journey begin!

ACT FOUR
Middle Age

Scene 1: Karla asks for a divorce

The middle of my life snuck up on me. Having generally good health, and looking younger than my calendar years, I was shocked on one fine Saturday several decades ago when a young man who had parked his car near mine said, "Move your car, old man!" Surely, he must have meant my father or perhaps some older gentleman standing behind me.

No, this young whippersnapper meant me, the rapidly-aging former shortstop. I knew with my head, but not my heart, that I could not remain a child forever. The pressures of time and circumstance almost require us to grow up. My life was no exception to this caveat. As it is for all of us, the middle of my life was not entirely without some successes and certainly not without some pain, disappointments, and conflicts.

It started as an ordinary day, but then… Karla said to me in the privacy of our bedroom, "I want a divorce!" I was incredulous, shocked. I still recall how stern, angry, and serious she looked. After all, my mom and dad stayed together, and it seemed that their lives had been far worse. Regardless of circumstances, they stuck together and somehow managed to make their relationship work. Up to this point, I had no idea Karla and I were in trouble as a couple.

Why did she want out? I am not even sure she knew why she wanted the marriage to end. I wondered, had she had an affair, and wanted to justify it in some way? Had she found someone else? And if she had an affair, did she think that you only had sex with people you were married to, as I had thought decades earlier? I begged her to tell me why—"Why do you want out?" Did I think if I knew the reason(s), I could fix things? She refused to answer this important question.

Over the next few weeks and months, we continued to live together, but we argued nearly every day. I kept trying to find out what was wrong, and what I needed to do to keep us together. But she remained so very angry whenever we spoke. For how many years had she been holding back her anger? Finally, months later, she gave me a reason for ending our lives together. In an angry outburst, she blurted out, "It's because you never bought me a microwave oven!" Of course, I know now that a kitchen appliance did not cause our breakup. Still, to this day, I don't know exactly what happened to the "us" that had been. Desperate, I asked her, "Do you still love me?" Her response was short and not sweet. "I love you like a brother." Those words sting me even forty years later.

To this very day, it is too painful for me to go further into this exploration. Suffice it to say, we did get a legal divorce in the mid-1980s. It was a contentious and not at all amicable parting of the ways. I did not want to divorce. Karla seemed intent on leaving me as quickly as possible. Still, she may have struggled with her final decision as late as the day before we were to appear in divorce court.

By this time, I had a new job at a local hospital doing educational training for its employees. Hoping to save the marriage, I had quit the job I loved so that I could be gone from home more. Earlier, Karla had told me that I was under her feet too much, and that I should get a regular (translation: 40 to 50 hours per week) job. I did so, but without any resulting change in her plans for the ending of our marriage.

At 9:00 a.m. of the fateful day of the legal divorce hearing, I was sitting in my dungeon-like office in the basement of the 1916-built health care facility for Cleveland's poor. My soon-to-be-former-wife telephoned me asking plaintively, "Do you think we should really go through with this? ... because I am not so positive about divorcing."

After the many months I suffered knowing that the love of my life was about to take up a new life without me, I was infuriated at her question. I responded almost without thinking about the repercussions of what I was about to say to her. "Oh," I began sarcastically. "I guess I must have misunderstood you after all those passing months. I actually thought you wanted a divorce." Sometimes I speak without properly thinking of the consequences of my words. This was one of those times.

In the late 1980s, on a cold day in March, our marriage was

officially over. But, the relationship was not. Robert Anderson, in his play, *I Never Sang For My Father*, says in the prologue, "Death ends a life, but not a relationship which struggles on in the minds of the survivors toward some resolution which it never finds," or words to that effect. Anderson was right on the money with regard to parent-child connections. But what he may not have known was that the same caveat appears to be true for a divorced couple. Our children are now grown and have children of their own but, especially around the holidays, there is plenty of time available to rehash unresolved issues and hurts. Maybe, just maybe, time does *not* heal all wounds after all.

Scene 2: Angst and profligate behavior

Some months ago, in an effort to help me prepare to write this memoir, I was asked to identify a memory I try not to think about. Further, "Why do you reject it? Was it painful? Embarrassing? Humiliating? Frightening? Write as if no one but you will ever read these words." Then finally, I was told to "Write a lot about this memory." The results of this little exercise are included here.

When I was first divorced in the 1980s, I felt devastated and confused. I also felt worthless. The woman I loved had rejected me—the split was entirely her idea. Even our wedding rings spoke about our hopes and dreams for the marriage. Inside my ring was inscribed the words, "With Karla to God." And on the interior of her ring, the inscription read, "With Steven to God." It seems we were serious about staying together. We had been married for 16 years at the time of the divorce, and we had two children together, a son and a daughter.

I did not know where to turn or who to turn to in my state of craziness following the break-up. As a licensed professional clinical counselor, I have been cautioned numerous times to not use the pejorative word "crazy" or its counterpart "craziness" as they are demeaning to counseling clients. Yet, I am sure that those words were appropriate to me during and after the marital break-up.

Looking back on those first few months, I do believe I was so grief-stricken, so distraught that I thought my life was over. It seemed that there was no one and nothing for me, except for my own wits. My former wife and I had had joint legal and physical custody of the children. Perhaps having joint custody helped to make my adjustment even more difficult. Meeting my own needs proved to be stressful enough, without having to care for children as well. Still, I tried as best as I could to give my children what they needed, but I am afraid I failed them, my pain was so central to my daily life.

I felt like I was dying or perhaps already dead, at least emotionally. And I was ever so lonely without my partner. The more she got her life together—new husband, new baby—the worse I felt. What was I to do? One thing I did not do was to keep up my nutrition. I had no appetite at all, and I stopped eating. I lost a full twenty pounds in the aftermath of the breakup. Barely a month after my wife told me that she wanted out of the marriage, my former high school held a reunion. Of course, my soon-to-be ex refused to go. I went anyway. At the reunion, a former classmate told me how awful I looked. I burst into quiet tears. I gave John a brief summary of the recent events in my life. He was not someone I had ever confided in before, but I felt desperate to tell someone—probably hoping I could get some answers to what was happening to me, or at least get some solid advice. My classmate was at a loss for words. Years later, I saw him again. To his credit he remembered the events from a decade earlier. And he asked me how I was doing now. I could honestly say I was doing reasonably well.

If I could find no help, no answers from former classmates or from the career change I made earlier, where could I turn? Alcohol did not help—my experiences with my alcoholic father had prevented me from seeking total solace in a bottle. Besides, I knew my children still needed a sober and fully-present father.

My short-sighted answer was to turn to relationships or rather to sex. I was not interested in a long-term connection with a woman—I was much too wounded for that. Instead, it was the warmth and tenderness of another human body that I craved. After much thought, I decided to place an advertisement in one of those "lonely-hearts" magazines. If I could not have the woman I had loved, at least I could try to console myself with sheer volume.

And volume I found. I do not recall what I said in the advertisements (I ran the solicitation more than once). But, I had lots of responses. And I replied to every one of them. Although today I cannot remember a single one of the first or last names of any of these women, I did my best to win the affection and approval of all of them. It was like a 21st century romantic comedy movie, only without any real romance and with very little laughter. I met women at restaurants, at bars, at coffee shops, and at museums—anywhere they would agree to meet with me.

There must have been dozens and dozens of women—some perhaps as lonely and as hurt as I was. I am not proud of my behavior. In fact, I am ashamed and embarrassed at how I acted. Not interested in most of the women personally, I sought only my own gratification and relief from the pain I felt.

Looking back now, I realize that I did not see the women as people, with their own issues and problems, but rather as salve for my open wounds. What a disservice I did to them! Yet, perhaps some of the women were using me in the same way as I used them. In any case, I hope I did not emotionally hurt any of these women during my state of confusion. If I did, I hope they will someday forgive me. I am still trying to forgive myself for my foolish actions. I have no valid excuse for my behavior, and I regret how I behaved.

There is also a possibility that one or more of these "partners" became pregnant. I still sometimes wonder if there is a grown-up child somewhere looking for her/his father—for me. There is no way to know if such a child exists. But, I am announcing here that I am available to be found. And I can provide offended parties access to discuss the situation with me. Even those statements sound weak and pitiful to me. Again, I ask for forgiveness for my actions or the lack of appropriate actions, and for any harm I may have caused to any child born thanks to my frivolousness.

Given this report of my callous sexual behavior, it seems surprising to me and probably to others, that religion played an important part in my childhood and on into my adulthood. I am going out on a limb here to say that guilt is not always inappropriate. In my case, guilt has served to remind me of my poor behavior and to suggest to me that I am not always as innocent or blame-free as I told myself at the time. *Mea culpa, mea maxima culpa* (translation: I really, really screwed up). And I do not intend any play on words here.

Scene 3: Pain that may never end: Karla gets remarried

My world turned upside down (again) the day that a neighbor said to me, "Did you hear? Your wife is getting married next week." I think I acted nonchalantly before this neighbor, but inside I felt shocked. My own children did not tell me about this planned event. Surely they must have known the effect this revelation would have on me. Perhaps they kept quiet out of concern that the news would hurt me. And it did. She would soon marry one of her co-workers at her hospital just one year after our divorce. I thought that she and I had married for a lifetime, yet here she was saying "I do" to someone else. Surprisingly, her new partner practiced a religion outside her own faith. She used to refer to me as her "dear Catholic man." Apparently, she no longer needed religious support for her own faith.

Dashed now was any hope I had that we could get back together. As if to add an exclamation point to the end of my hopes for reconciliation, she also had a baby with her new spouse less than a year after her second marriage. I had begged her to have another child with me, but to no avail. It is only my theory, but I believe she could scarcely wait to have a child with her new beau.

Making these statements about my former wife reminds me of another incident that took place years before my divorce. Briefly, I had a "conversation" with an unborn child. I was driving south on Interstate 71, a highway that runs between Cleveland, Ohio and Louisville, Kentucky and no further.

I may have been heading to Kentucky to do more genealogical research on my mother's family. Libraries in both Frankfurt and

Louisville have excellent records, some original, for researching Kentucky and Virginia forebears. In any case, I was driving alone having left behind my wife and children for a few days.

Suddenly, out of nowhere came a perceived voice—that of a little girl. I did not so much hear a real physical voice as a series of loud thoughts, for lack of a better phrase. The female voice said, and I swear this incident is true, although I am paraphrasing here, "Daddy, daddy? It's me, Sarah Elizabeth. I'm your daughter. Please help me be born. If you don't help me, I will never be alive." I am a bit afraid of being judged for recounting this experience, but this did happen to me over 35 years ago. Surprisingly, at the time, I did not think that this event was other-worldly. It seemed to me a perfectly natural experience. Upon arriving at home, I repeated this same story to my then-wife. She had little to say about my tale, except to say something like, "Oh, how interesting." Sarah Elizabeth was right. I did not help, nor did my spouse cooperate. So Sarah is but a name in a somewhat interesting story. If she had ever lived she would now be about 37 years old. I wonder what Sarah would be like. Would she have had children of her own? Sadly, I will not get an answer to these questions.

One thing I can take away from the Sarah tale is that it seems to me that *family* is exceptionally important to me. I yearn to belong, to be connected in an intimate way. So, it is little wonder that I still feel hurt more than three decades after the divorce, Karla's remarriage, and the birth of her late-life child. Unfortunately, having two children with my first wife almost forces me to face my various losses again and again.

For example, I recently visited my son and two of my grandchildren. I arrived at his Florida home to see a package lying on the kitchen counter. The package contained a birthday gift and card from my former wife for our grandson. Worse, Karla's new married name appeared on the package's return address label. Ouch! What a painful mess life can be! I am not the first in my family to suffer such losses, and unfortunately, I will not be the last.

One of my great-grandmothers, Elizabeth Underwood, was a pioneer in divorce. Elizabeth (1632-1673) was the third daughter of William Underwood and Margaret Mason. Her parents were wealthy landowners in Jamestown colony in what is now the state of Virginia.

Elizabeth made history of a sort in the Virginia colony. She was married to Dr. James Taylor, a Virginia physician. In the early 1650s, Elizabeth filed a petition with the Governor of the colony and his Council. In it she pleaded for a legal separation and divorce from Taylor. There had been rumors of abuse on the doctor's part. On March 26, 1654, the Governor granted Elizabeth an official divorce.

Supposedly, this legal divorce was the very first to be granted in Virginia--thus leading to Elizabeth's claim to fame. Still, Elizabeth went on to marry a total of four times before her death in 1673. By the time she died, her official name was Elizabeth Underwood Catlett Taylor Slaughter Butler. All direct descendants of William Underwood, including my grandmother, Mary J. Underwood, are eligible for membership in the *Jamestowne Society*. This organization accepts those who can demonstrate a direct tie to the first settlers in Jamestown, Virginia during the period 1600-1700.

Scene 4: Meeting Sheila

I am quite pleased to say that my middle years have not all been a story of misfortune, misery, and pain. Some events and adventures have even helped me to at least partially heal from a few of my earlier difficulties. For instance, on a quiet February evening in the 1980s, I picked up my date for that night—a secretary from a suburban school--that I had met as a result of one of the advertisements I had placed in the "lonely hearts" classifieds of a local magazine. I think the ad may have said something like "Desperate bachelor with a fine sense of humor needs some fun to forget his troubles," or some equally silly pleading for love and affection.

She answered my plea, Darlene did. I have no idea what her last name was, and I barely remember her as being a few years younger than me, divorced, and with dark hair. Her height and weight were in proportion to each other. She was attractive, but I knew from the start that this relationship was going nowhere that resembled anything serious. I was right.

I picked her up in one of those small, sporty-looking, but cheaply made coupes, probably at her house in the same Cleveland suburb where she worked. From there, we went straight to a night club cum bar for an evening of dancing and listening to music from the '50s and '60s in between interruptions by a disc jockey. In my fantasy, the DJ's other job was as a bartender at some ethnic tavern or perhaps as a day laborer for some non-descript construction company. This is my way of saying that the Hilton nightclub's disc jockey was not very talented.

About an hour or so into the evening, I noticed a couple at a nearby table. I am not sure what was remarkable about them, but something drew my eyes toward this duo. I did notice that they seemed to be uncomfortable or at least not pleased with how their respective evenings were transpiring. Perhaps that was simply a projection on my part since I was not having the best of times with Darlene. I later discovered that the man had been drinking excessively, and simultaneously annoying his date.

Just a short time later, the male member of this couple wandered over to my table, and looked directly at Darlene. Boldly, he asked her if she would dance with him. I suppose he thought we were not having the time of our lives (he was correct) and sensed no jealousy or threat from me. Darlene looked back imploringly at me as if to say, "I am with you, kid. What do you think of this offer?"

I could think of no reason why he should not take Darlene off my hands for this dance or for the entire evening for that matter. Truthfully, we were not exactly enamored of each other anyway. My date got up and she and her temporary partner began to fast dance, perhaps to a Smoky Robinson or Diana Ross pre-recorded number.

I am not sure what Darlene and the interloper had to say to each other during their spin around the dance floor. But, in my version of a now humorous and fortuitous story, I spoke to the interloper's date, asking her name and if she would like to join me at my table. When Sheila (the interloper's companion) tells this story now, it is I who asked her if she would grant me an audience with her at her table. The devil seems to be in the details!

Either way, I found out her name, and that she was a nursing student at a nearby college. In fact, we did a little name dropping, and she revealed to me that we had a mutual acquaintance at the hospital at which I was now working. I had quit my teaching job a few months earlier and had begun to train a local hospital's employees.

It is my understanding that after some discussion between Sheila and my colleague, the two of them decided it would be acceptable for the colleague to give me Sheila's telephone number. Darlene re-entered this drama when she later informed me that although it was obvious that I was attracted to Sheila, "She is just not right for you." So much for Darlene's errant prognostications!

No, this tale does not have a story-book, "and-from-that-moment-forward- they-lived-happily-ever-after" kind of ending. But still, the story is a very pleasant one. Sheila has three sons and I have both a son and a daughter. All the children are within a few years of each other. But, the reality is that blended families have lots of adjustment problems on average. Our two families were no exception.

I probably had more difficulty adjusting to her children than she had in making accommodations for mine. Truthfully, I was the one who wavered about whether we should join families. At least, that was true in the beginning. Eventually, even Sheila had serious misgivings about creating a new blended family, turning down my suggestions for a marriage on more than one occasion.

After almost four years of dating, we finally decided to make our relationship official and legal. On as warm spring day in the late 1980s, we were married by a Catholic priest, not in a church, but at Sheila's house. An unusual setting for a Catholic wedding to be sure, but I was both pleased and frightened at the start of my new life.

My second marriage was sanctioned by the Catholic Church because my first wife had applied for and received an *annulment* from the Church probably on the grounds that she was too young to know what she was doing at the time she married me (she was just shy of twenty-one years old).

In the Catholic Church, an annulment is the judgment by a Church court (called a *tribunal*) that a marriage previously thought to be valid failed to contain one or more of the elements deemed to be necessary for a binding and valid marriage. (http://www.usccb.org/issues-and-action/marriage/annulment? Retrieved 11-27-2017.)

Marriages are considered valid by the Catholic Church if: the spouses are free to marry, both parties are capable of giving their consent to marry, they do freely give their consent to the other, intend to be open to having children, intend to marry for life, intend to be faithful to each other, and their respective consents are given in front of two witnesses and an authorized Church minister. https://en.wikipedia.org/wiki/Declaration_of_nullity Retrieved 11-27-2017.

Again, it was Karla who filed for the annulment, and I now believe she did so because she intended to marry again and wanted the Church's blessing on her new relationship. At the tribunal's urging, she had documents sent my house, offering me the opportunity to respond to her annulment application. And I did so by completing a very long and very personal questionnaire.

Interestingly, the spouse who is not applying for the annulment does NOT need to agree that the marriage was never valid for the declaration of nullity to occur. If the Church tribunal agrees with the applicant that a valid marriage was not contracted, the other party has no recourse. Also fascinating to me is the fact that it took sixteen years of marriage and the birth of two children for my former spouse and the Church to decide our marriage was invalid. The reasoning behind this remains a mystery to me to this day. Needless to say, it is my belief that both of us had met all of the requirements of the Catholic Church to create a valid and committed union. The Church disagreed.

I still feel unsettled about the fact that in the opinion of a Church court I was never validly married to my first wife. I am also still upset that my beliefs about my commitment to my former spouse and to the sacrament of marriage were irrelevant in the Church's decision. In any case though, I am pleased to be married to Sheila. Marrying someone that I love, and who professes to love me has gone a long way in helping me to heal from the pain of my losses.

Sheila has become my best friend, and is almost certainly the best friend I have ever had. We do not agree on everything, and we manage to find various ways to express our dissatisfaction in the behavior of the other. In short, ours is not a perfect union. But, it is a good one. It is a pleasure to have a committed partner with whom to share the joys and the difficulties of life with in a supportive manner.

We have also become traveling partners, and have seen much of world together. Our joined lives are often a genuine adventure. For example, we have crawled inside the tunnels and darkened staircases of the pyramids and the pharaohs' tombs in the Valley of the Kings in Giza, Egypt. We have chased whales from a fishing boat off the coast of Costa Rica, and sailed the Nile River in a *felucca*. Not to be outdone in our water-borne adventures, we also swam in the fast-flowing Amazon River in Peru.

We have walked the streets of Istanbul, a town where one of my grandparents, Jeanne de Brienne, ruled as its Emperor (1229-1237) when it was known as *The Latin Empire of Constantinople*. Earlier in his royal career, Jeanne had also been the King of Jerusalem (1210-1225). Ironically, one of my grandmothers, Melisende, had been the Queen of Jerusalem in the previous century (1131-1153).

Finally, we have traveled to Poland where a newly-discovered cousin of mine, Slawek Chylinski, drove us all the way across that beautiful country in his rather elderly Toyota. With Slawek, we walked the same streets of the village of *Stare Rakowo* that my great, great, great, great grandfather, Piotr Chylinski strolled with his children and grandchildren in the late 1700s. What surrealistic adventures my partner and I have experienced! And even as we both age (gracefully, I might add), we still have many more places to see and to rejoice in.

Yet, the greatest adventure of all, at least for me, has occurred in the last four years following my retirement from teaching and counseling. Thanks to Sheila's generosity, I have been able to concentrate on an inward journey. She has continued to work at a full-time administrative job, while I have been free to explore my own identity by turning inward through self-exploration, researching my ancestors, and by writing about my discoveries. Thank you, Sheila.

It has been a joy to have so much time and support to do the things I have wanted to do for decades. Still, I am very aware of the passing of time. For example, I have stayed in touch with many of my high school classmates through telephone and e-mail correspondence. While I have enjoyed reminiscing with them about our respective youths, I have also taken notice of how many of the 144 graduates of Holy Name High School in Cleveland are no longer living. Gone are my friends and acquaintances such as Floyd "Spanky" Rybicki, Bob Ciesla, Pat Spisak, Margaret Mickey, Eric Truax, and Joe Scherma. I have known some of these people since I was twelve years old. Although I seldom saw most of them, except at organized class reunions, I have forever lost the opportunity to talk to them about the good old days when we were young and the world felt new and as fresh as a spring rainfall. It was a time when we were oh so innocent!

Late adulthood has a way of waking us up to the inevitable. Truth be told, I am even beyond late adulthood as the stages of my life pass so quickly. Although I am still healthy, I am now fast approaching old age, what sociologists now call "young-old." With true gallows humor, I translate this sociological term as, "You might feel or even look fairly young now, but just wait until you see what comes next!"

Scene 5: Not Catholic enough

I have taught college classes off and on since I was twenty-six years old. The classes have included in-person courses and online classes at five separate schools. All were public-supported institutions except one. That one exception was a Catholic college. The school was run by a group of priests and monks belonging to the Fontevrists, a Catholic order of religious founded in France during the Middle Ages. Incidentally, I have changed the name of the order of priests and monks who ran the school.

The Fontevrist order was not especially known for its academic prowess among academics themselves. Yet, this order and the school had a vaunted reputation for its "Catholic-ness." And by that term, I mean it was exceptionally conservative and quite orthodox in its views, much to the delight of the ultra-conservative papacy in Rome at that time.

Following my graduation with an advanced degree from a secular university, I began to apply for various college teaching jobs in my field. Amazingly, in a tight job market, I received positive responses from two schools simultaneously. One school was a public college and of course, non-sectarian, while the other was the conservative Catholic school.

I interviewed at both schools, and from the reactions I saw in the interviewers who were mostly professors and along with some administrators, I knew I would get a least one offer of employment. To my surprise, I got two.

Now, I was in a dilemma. Should I take the offer from the public college which had offered me not only a higher-paying teaching position, but hinted at an advance to an administrative appointment in the not-so-distant future? Or should I take the lower-paying offer from the Catholic school, remaining true to my Catholic roots and the faith of many of my ancestors on my father's side of the family?

Many colleges like to hire faculty at the lowest end of the pecking order of rank. The lowest rank is typically called *instructor*, while in ascending order of prestige (and salary), schools could also hire at the level of *assistant professor*, *associate professor*, or *professor*.

Hiring at the rank of instructor or even assistant professor can save a college thousands of dollars in salary over the years. Yet, some colleges prefer to hire at a higher rank in the hope of luring an especially attractive candidate to their doorstep. The public college's offer to me was at the rank of associate professor—one rung from the top level. The offer from the Catholic school was at the rank of assistant professor, and for a lower salary. That decision to hire at a lower rank was made not by the department chair who had seemed enamored with my candidacy, but by the college's dean—a fanatic and evangelizing Catholic.

I do not mean to bash the school or the dean involved. The dean did what he thought was best for the college. In fact, at the time I was hired, the dean also hired a "rival" psychology professor. Basically then, there were two of us hired for a single position. I suppose the dean expected me to fail miserably, leaving the position open for his choice. Things did not pan out for the dean. His selection for the psychology professorship flopped miserably. This psychology professor's reviews from his students were terrible. As a result, he was not granted tenure. In effect, a vote of non-tenure is a death knell to a teaching career, as the recipient receives no contract for the next school year.

In spite of my "victory" over my competition, I regret the choice of teaching positions I made to this very day. I elected to turn down the more prestigious and lucrative offer, going instead with the Fortevrist-led school. That choice was probably a mistake on my part. While I had wonderful reviews of my teaching from my students and the colleagues in my academic department, the administration seemed to look down upon me with disdain. For example, the then current dean regularly refused to make eye contact with me. When he was forced by circumstances to speak with me, he put great effort into not smiling or showing other nonverbal signs of approval.

Why? Apparently, it was because I was not the "right" kind of

Catholic. I attended Mass and received the sacraments regularly, but I was anything but a proselytizing, evangelical fanatic about my faith. Catholics are not alone when it comes to subgroups within its community of believers. In Judaism, there are also several classes of believers, although I do not know how much, if any, animosity there is between the groups of orthodox, conservative, and liberal practitioners of that faith. But, I suspect that if I had identified with the Jewish faith, I would have opted to join a liberal congregation.

During my time teaching at the Catholic school, I often thought that the institution would have been more comfortable as a seminary for the training of priests. In fact, those who taught religion or Catholic philosophy were possibly members of the school's highest paid department. Certainly, the most prestigious group was the Theology department. Overall, the school was not open to fully accepting "ordinary" academics and researchers as equals, not even those who practiced the Catholic faith. And heaven help those who were closet atheists or agnostics. These professors (and I knew a few of them personally) had to spend their work time in emotional and intellectual hiding, seldom mentioning their beliefs except to trusted friends.

I do not say these things about some of the school's faculty and administrators because I thought they were "bad" people. Nor do I believe that that the vast majority of employees and students were anything but honest and sincere people who loved their faith. I am sure they were both.

But, my point here is that I soon realized that I made a mistake when I hired on at this college. Based on their nonverbal behavior, the top-level administration of the college, the president and academic dean included, was not enamored of me. I frequently had the sense that I was being *scrutinized* in some way. Yes, I know this sounds paranoid. And I am the first to admit that I do run slightly paranoid in my daily life even now. But, whatever behaviors I saw or heard that led me to believe I was being judged, seemed real to me. And in any case, colleges typically pride themselves in giving "academic freedom" to their faculty, meaning the teachers could feel relatively comfortable in their research and in their classrooms. The Fontevrists offered only freedom within certain very narrow limits.

I was not the only faculty member who had a sense of being closely observed (and judged) by the administration. In fact, I know of three cases in which faculty left the school after only a short stay at the college. In one case, a Catholic priest, Fr. John Filson, left his teaching position abruptly at the end of his first year. In my fantasy, he left either because he was asked to leave or because he felt a discomfort similar to mine. Anyway, it seems that in Fr. John's experience, there are priests and then there are the "good" priests (read: conservative and very orthodox). Apparently, all Catholics are not made alike.

In the second case, Sean O'Brien, a philosophy department faculty and a Catholic, left after two years. During his second and final year at the college, he confided in me that he was gay. While he laughed when he revealed this to me, I could not help but think that he feared he was also being carefully scrutinized. Perhaps, Sean wanted to avoid the embarrassment of a potential discovery of his sexual preferences. Surely, a conservative and orthodox school could not have tolerated such a faculty member.

In the final instance, Laura Jamison, although she was a practicing Catholic, simply disappeared as her initial contract to teach expired. She later turned up at a private university where I just happened to be doing a bit of consulting. Although I know she recognized me, she turned away each time I approached her to talk about the "good old days." I never did make peace with Laura. But, in my fantasy, I believe she might have thought I was one of the bad guys—the scrutinizing judges from her past.

Eventually, I left the Catholic college. I now enjoy a much greater sense of freedom than I thought I had in that job. And on a more optimistic note, I think I positively influenced some students and perhaps even a few of the school's administrators. At least, I hope I made a strong impact. Toward the end of my time at the school, I spoke informally to the same dean who had insisted that if the department chair felt he absolutely must hire me, he would have to do so at a low rank and at a very low salary. But, I am getting ahead of my story about my final days at the school. Read on to see how that interchange with the dean transpired.

In fairness to that college, I will say that after seven short years, I was granted tenure—meaning that barring an economic catastrophe, I could count on keeping my position for as long as I chose. In fact, I became so successful at the school that I was offered tenure by two separate departments, Psychology and Education. While my doctorate is in psychology, I also hold a Masters' degree in Urban Education. Finally, I was promoted to a full professorship after 12 years at the school. There was not much debate about that final promotion as my teaching reviews generated by my students were quite flattering.

Near my retirement from teaching at the Catholic college, I came upon the dean in the administration's area of offices. He shook my hand and said, "It looks like I was wrong about you." I was so taken aback by his comment that I could scarcely mutter, "Thank you." Thinking back on that event now, I wished I had pursued that line of discussion with the dean in more depth. I regret that I did not. That was as close to an apology as I ever received for what I perceived as biased treatment, especially during the initial hiring process.

I realize that if I did not feel appreciated at this institution, I had the obligation to find other work. After all, once the school's ultra-conservative mission became clear to me, and that I did not quite fit there, I could have left and found other work. I accept responsibility for not doing just that.

Still, there were some benefits to working there. As an added bonus to the tolerable salary I eventually received, I used my position as a means to continue my family research. I estimate that in my spare time at that institution, I completed as much as 50% of the data-gathering I would use to write five or six articles on various ancestors and historical characters from my family tree. As a college teacher, research and writing are considered part of the work. These two categories were used by administrators each year to partially determine the pay increase for the next school year.

Dutifully, I listed my research and my writing on the evaluation forms I was required to complete near the end of each academic year. To my pleasant surprise, I regularly received positive evaluations not only from my teaching efforts, but from my contributions to the academic literature too.

I am sure that somewhere the seven Catholic saints and single Protestant saint that I have since discovered in my family tree must be rejoicing in my accomplishments. I just don't know if the source of their joy is that I identified them by name and that I have told their life stories or if they are celebrating over my leaving that religious school. In any case, I salute all of my ancestors. Native Americans, it is said, thank the animals they have trapped or killed for freely giving themselves up to their hunters or captors. In a similar way, I thank these ancestors for revealing themselves to me.

Scene 6: Down under, South American-style

The middle age portion of this memoir would not be complete without some tales of travel during those years. While much of my mid-life was a period of upheaval, my years with my second wife, Sheila, were laced with contentment, a pinch of struggle, and a heavy heaping of adventure. There were the several trips to Venezuela for no other reason than to finally see the South American continent. And how could I forget the trips to Europe with all five of our children? Then, perhaps intruding on Act Five (Old Age) of this tome, there were the trips to Scandinavia, Poland, Turkey, and the safari in the Republic of South Africa. But, it is a memorable journey to Peru that is the subject of the next few paragraphs.

Sometime in the late 1980s, I spent an enjoyable winter's day studying a map of the world and I suppose some old *National Geographic* magazines. My goal: to find somewhere exotic to visit for our delayed honeymoon. Near the top of our respective travel-related bucket lists were several trips to South American destinations. Peru appeared on each of our south-of-the-Equator dream vacations. Yet, we were only vaguely aware of the newspaper and television news stories coming out of southern Peru. Rebel troops were fighting in the mountains against Peruvian government troops. The most feared of these groups was the *Sendero Luminoso*, AKA, The Shining Path.

The Shining Path was a Marxist terrorist group whose goal was to establish a dictatorship of the proletariat capable of initiating a world revolution, thus creating a pure communist state in contrast to what *Sendero's* leadership saw as revisionist socialist societies. Its tactics were simple—instigate terror and fear through murder and intimidation of locals, tourists, and especially government soldiers. The men and women of this revolutionary arm of the Communist

Party of Peru had as its immediate goal the overthrow of the federal government in Lima. (https://en.wikipedia Retrieved 1/15/2018.)

Still, we knew little of these dire circumstances until we arrived in Peru. Learning of these potential dangers, we were forced to alter some of our plans. Our revised itinerary called for us to avoid the famous archeological tourist site, Machu Pichu and the beautiful colonial city of Cusco--both located in far southeastern Peru. As for getting around the country (and avoiding trouble), we decided to travel by air on what we hoped were reliable Peruvian airlines, private taxis, and *collectivos*, a type of precursor to the modern passenger conveyance companies, Uber and Lyft. But instead of retrieving a couple or a single individual, *collectivos* would pick up multiple passengers, driving into out-of-the-way sites such as Indian villages to gather additional passengers.

Some of the details of the trip are a bit sketchy after the passing of nearly three decades, but I still recall this adventure with a good deal of excitement. We flew first into Miami, the heart of flights to Latin America. The MIA airport was chaotic to say the least. We must have heard at least three or four diverse languages being spoken as we traversed the great halls of the terminals.

We arrived in Lima, Peru via our non-stop flight from Miami on LanChile after a four or five hour flight. LanChile was the predecessor to Peru's current air carrier, LATAM Peru. The airport in Lima, Jorge Chavez International Airport, was even more chaotic than Miami's. I can vaguely recall a very smooth flight across a portion of the Atlantic, the Caribbean Sea, the Central American landmass, and finally down the coast of the Pacific Ocean to the oceanfront capital of Peru.

Visitors to the airport, probably mostly locals, were not even allowed to enter the terminal. They were herded together by the hundreds just beyond a heavily-guarded fence between the sidewalk and the terminal building itself. I soon discovered that the favorite weapon of security personnel in Peru was not a .38 or .45 caliber sidearm, but a fully-automatic rifle that soldiers held in a constant, ready-to-fire position.

Amid this bustle were the inevitable tour hucksters and taxi drivers, and perhaps a few con men as well. Once again, there was shouting, pointing, gesticulating, and a calling out of passenger's names. *"Jorge, esta es papa!"* *"Magdalena, bienvenidos a Peru."* *"Tachsee,*

tachsee! Hey meester, you wanna tachsee?"

Bewildered at all this activity, we hired the first cab driver who could speak even a modicum of English. "Take us to the Hotel Kowabonga," we burst forth breathlessly. In truth that was not the name of the hotel that we had reserved before we left the United States. What I do recall about our lodgings in Lima was that our room was clean, the staff spoke passable English, and the barkeep served our new favorite alcoholic beverage in the hotel lobby bar—the Pisco sour. A couple of those sours ingested, we soon ignored our jet-lag-induced exhaustion and stress, and our unfamiliarity with this south-of-the-Equator culture. We asked for adventure, and we were in store for more than we had planned. For those who have not had the pleasure of ingesting a pisco sour, it is considered the national drink of both Peru and Chile.

The Peruvian version is made of a light-colored brandy, which is distilled from wine, freshly-squeezed lime juice, syrup, ice, egg whites, and Angostura bitters. The online erstwhile encyclopedia, *wikipedia.com*, devotes ten full pages, including references and a bibliography, to the subject. Apparently, booze is very important to Peruvian culture.

The history of the drink is rather intriguing. It is the brainchild of an American expatriate to Peru, Victor Vaughen Morris. Morris came to work in Cerro de Pasco, a town in central Peru in 1903. Tiring of life in the back waters of the country, Morris relocated to Lima where he opened a bar in 1916. His enterprise was initially quite successful as his trademark drink soon garnered a glowing reputation among his primary customers, the elite of Lima and English-speaking foreigners.

Morris himself had apparently guzzled more than a few pisco sours, as he died of cirrhosis of the liver in 1929. At the time of his death, Morris' famous drink was a mere ten years old. He would have no way of knowing that he had started a national craze in both Peru and Chile. (https://en.wikipedia.org/Pisco_sour Retrieved 1/22/2018.)

While the national drink of Peru was a bit of a pleasant surprise to my wife Sheila and I, the weather on the day of our arrival proved to be equally unpleasant. We had read numerous travel books about Peru before our journey so as to minimize surprises, but we had anticipated the weather to be California-style—warm, clear, and dry with low humidity. We were wrong and so apparently were the original Spanish conquerors of this region.

A tale is told about Peru's early history. Initially, the newly-discovered area was a blank space on European maps. The conquistadors must have been concerned about where to administer this territory from because they soon turned to the natives for advice on an appropriate site for the conquered lands' capital. Probably laughing into their sleeves (or more likely into their bare arms), the original locals suggested the beautiful countryside of modern-day central Peru as the aspiring nation's capital. The joke was at the expense of the Spaniards. Located in a mini-climate not dissimilar to San Francisco in the United States, Lima is the recipient of many cloudy or at least foggy and chilly days. Everywhere we went in our few days in Lima we hoped to find a working fireplace, somewhere we could escape the damp chill of the "tropics." We soon beat a hasty retreat from Lima as we hoped to warm ourselves. Truthfully, Peru's capital was not a whole lot warmer than a moderate winter's day in Cleveland, Ohio—our home.

In our pre-travel research on Peru, we had learned of the existence of a town and a warmer area of Peru called the Paracas Peninsula. In fact, one of the main towns of the Peninsula was also called Paracas. So we hired a taxi driver and his vehicle for the three or four-hour drive from Lima down the well-known Pan American Highway to our previously-reserved oceanfront hotel in Paracas.

What we did not know at the time was that the highway was a dangerous place at any time of the day. Not only could there be highwaymen lurking behind boulders and abandoned buildings, but the police were nearly as shifty as the criminals. I am not sure why we left for Paracas so late in the day, but we found ourselves on the nearly-empty Highway at nightfall. Strangely, our driver drove without headlights or even parking lights. He could not speak English, but I gathered from his gesticulating that it was best not to announce our presence by showing any signs of life. My heart began to beat more quickly, and I thought to myself but did not say out loud, "If I do have a fatal heart attack now, I can make a major contribution to the driver's desire to show little sign of life in our vehicle!"

Thankfully, we were not accosted by thieves on our way to Paracas. The hotel we had reserved consisted of a series of small cottages and nicely-landscaped grounds. I remember only snippets about our stay on the Peninsula and in the town. There was the smell of the fish processing factory immediately next door to the hotel. If the wind was just right, I found myself guessing which species of fish was being sliced, diced, and canned for someone's dinner or more likely from the aroma, for cat food.

There was also the memorable ride in a *collectivo*. We were one of the early passengers in the late-model van, and so we sat in the middle section of the vehicle to better accommodate later arrivals. We were headed into the town of Paracas for what we hoped would be a satisfying dinner. The driver took a dusty side road that ended in an even dustier driveway that led to a native seaside village.

Stopping at the ocean's edge and in the heart of the village, we took on a handful of new passengers who appeared to be from a single family. By this time, we were all cramped tightly together like sardines (if you will pardon the fish factory humor). Nearest to me was a small boy, perhaps five years old. Seeing him wobble and sway with his eyes closing, I began to wonder what his nighttime sleeping arrangements were. Then, he went a step further to alleviate his exhaustion. He gently laid his head on my lap, and fell asleep instantly while standing. Everyone who saw these actions smiled simultaneously as if we had shared a tender moment. We had.

What I have not mentioned was that I was wearing a pair of fashionable, resort-style, ultra-white trousers. Let me say here the pants had been perfectly clean before I became a human pillow on that mini-bus. Even so, I am pleased to have had this intimate moment with this beautiful little child.

Our stay in Paracas at an end, we were shocked to see the same taxi driver arrive at our hotel to escort us back to Lima for further adventures. He had promised to do so, but as an American accustomed to surly and unpredictable cab drivers, I was greatly pleased to see him again. Still, our return to Lima provided us with another adventure-filled story.

We were perhaps halfway back on our northward-bound trek to the capital city, when we noticed a highway patrol car heading south on the Pan American Highway. But, instead of continuing to drive south, the patrol car's driver looked intently at our taxi, and made a quick U-turn. The patrol car began to follow us closely. I don't recall if the highway patrolmen flashed their lights at us or blew their vehicle's horn, but our driver knew to pull to the side of the road. Both highway patrolmen exited their car, with each brandishing one of those automatic weapons in the "Beware, my friend, I-am-ready-to-use-this" stance.

Initially, they took the driver to the rear of his cab, gesturing for him to raise his trunk lid. I imagined the officers did those things to obscure our vision of the impending transaction. I believe I was correct since Peruvian *intis* left the pocket of the driver, and rested softly in the hands of one of the gentlemen from the "law." Mostly satisfied with their take, the officers then roamed around the cabbie's vehicle, staring intently into the back seat where we were seated. The men were not smiling as they gave us what I imagined were hungry stares. The *patrulla de carreteras* left satisfied that there was no more profit to be had.

At this point of our honeymoon, we longed for still more exciting times. Sitting in bed of the room at our original hotel back in Lima, I began to make telephone calls trying to find someone who would arrange a side trip to the Amazon jungle for us for the next day. After all, why travel so close to one of the wonders of the natural world without experiencing *La Selva*?

From the hotel's concierge, I had a few telephone numbers of Lima travel agents who specialized in jungle outings. Finding an agent who could deliver to us Peruvian airline tickets and vouchers for a boat trip up the Amazon River, I began to haggle for a better price. Sheila, anxious to book a trip to the wilds, shook her head violently, as she wanted me to buy an arranged trip without further talk. The agent and I agreed on a price and arranged to meet the next morning.

What I did not know then was that he could assure us only of seats on a flight *to* Iquitos, a frontier city and the jumping off point for Amazon adventures, but which had little else to offer. We had tickets for return flights to Lima, but we had no guarantee we would leave the jungle in a timely way. Young and rather foolish, we took the deal even without assurances of seats on a return flight.

The flight to Iquitos itself was spectacular. Flying on a locally-owned, small airline's propeller-driven McDonald-Douglas aircraft, we soon found ourselves at 25,000 feet barely clearing the crests of the Andes Mountains, that great chain of ruggedness that runs from the southern tip of the South American continent to the edge of Venezuela in the north. I was both transfixed and frightened to be in this real-life, Disney-style ride in what appeared to be a thirty-year-old aircraft flown by a now-defunct airline.

Needless to say, we arrived safely in Iquitos. Let's just say that Indiana Jones, the fictitious star of the adventure film, *Raiders of the Lost Ark*, would have felt right at home in that city. Founded by rubber barons in the previous century, Iquitos was the quintessential frontier town. It was everything the jungle promised to be--hot, humid, run-down, with a steady air of excitement for those willing to challenge *la Selva*.

Walking across dusty streets, passing pedestrians outfitted to the hilt like movie extras, and dodging pedi-cabs powered by bicycles, we soon found our way to the River and to our tour director. The travel agent's representative was a young man in his early twenties. He could speak some English, but seemed lost if we spoke too quickly.

Taking on a few more passengers into our flimsy-looking craft, we motored perhaps fifty miles upriver to a landing that housed our camp, *Amazon Lodge*. The lodge consisted of a handful of cabins attached to each other by a wooden walkway. They were comfortable enough, but let me say here and now, they were not luxurious in any way. There was no attached restaurant, no lobby, and no swimming pool, only a central meeting area for the guests to eat at makeshift outdoor tables.

Our guide, whom I shall call Felipe, did all of the cooking. Using both fresh fish he caught earlier in the day and supplies he brought with him when we left Iquitos, he cooked up some tasty meals for our small group of jungle explorers. Not only did Felipe cook well, he could also play the guitar. For some reason, Felipe took a liking to me, and even made up a song using my name at the evening campfire. We were destined to make additional contact the next day.

Most of the guests, including Sheila and I, wandered down to the river the next morning. Felipe, ever the adventurer, said in broken English that he would jump into the river if he had human company. I demurred, saying I had seen enough adventure movies to know that this body of water was filled with flesh-eating piranha.

Smiling, our guide managed to communicate with a series of grunts and gestures that there were no deadly fish in this part of the river. Since my mother did not raise any dummies, I told Felipe that if he went into the river first, then showed me that his skin was still intact, I would dive into the rushing waters after him. He jumped into the current, but on the pier side of our resting place. The current was so fast that if one missed grabbing the pier's pilings, he/she might be found days later upriver, perhaps in the mouth of an alligator or other jungle creature with large teeth.

I followed Felipe into the raging waters, and obviously after a few minutes in the drink, I caught enough of the wooden pilings to survive unharmed. I don't believe I would take such a swim today, but I was young and adventurous then.

The following day we went to the airport in Iquitos, unsure we would be able to catch a flight that day or ever for that matter. After all, we had tickets, but had no guarantee of a seat. It was then that I was introduced to the third world strategy for customer service. In this case, that service consisted of everyone racing all at once to the ticket counter helter-skelter hoping to garner the attention of the service representative by speaking loudly.

At first I tried to be polite, guessing at when it would be my turn to inquire about seats. That turn never came, so I bought into the third world system, and began shouting at the clerk, "Sir, I need two seats on the next (and only) flight to Lima." Perhaps confused by my lack of discernible Spanish and my garbled English, I got his attention, and acquired two of the last seats on this flight to civilization. We would soon be back in Lima's modernity, and in twenty-four more hours, back in the United States. While I am not grandiosely patriotic, I have always treasured returning to my home country. I seldom realize how stressful foreign travel can be until the stress disappears. Seeing the American flag and hearing American accents for the first time puts a grand smile on my face no matter how little or long I have been gone.

ACT FIVE
Old Age

Scene 1: Illness and belief: Chlotilde & Clovis revisited

It was a relief to find out that my son would live after all. His wife called to tell me that he was admitted to a medical ward of an out-of-state hospital, and that he had been placed in the intensive care unit. I did not know what that meant for Sean. Why was he placed in the intensive care unit? Why was he in the hospital in the first place? All that his wife could tell me that he was deathly ill.

I just knew I had to go see him for myself. Since he was married, I could not get substantial information from the hospital staff over the telephone. Of course, I was now no longer my son's next of kin. And because of Federal regulations, his caregivers would not give me any personal or even identifying information. Flooded with worry about my son, I booked a flight to an airport near his hospital for the very next day.

Walking into his hospital room, I was aghast at how ill he looked. His eyes were blackened and he had a wide, red ring encircling his neck. Someone on the hotel staff—he was staying there as a guest while he was on an out-of-town business trip—had found him in his hotel room in dire need of help. He was taken to the nearest hospital by ambulance. He and his wife were having personal problems that I had been unaware of, and these social issues were exacerbated by the fact that he had developed the early stages of diabetes. Apparently, his pancreas was shutting down, unable to effectively produce or process insulin.

In the original draft of this book, I had planned to say how pleased I was that my son seemed to have made a full recovery from the near fatal damage to his pancreas that was caused by the undetected diabetes. While I was relieved that my son appeared to be well again, I was still worried that his diabetes or that the earlier damage to his pancreas might return. As of a few weeks ago, Sean was readmitted to the hospital with the same problems he had originally.

While he will likely survive this reoccurrence of illness, he simply does not take good care of himself, physically or otherwise. I do not mean to sound cavalier or uncaring, but through this incident and others, I have come to realize that I cannot change anyone's behavior or even manage someone's diet, no matter who the person is or how destructive his/her behavior is.

You must understand that when I make this detached statement, à la *The Buddha*, I am trying to convince myself to think in this way. It is only a theory for me. In fact, this is a lesson that I must re-learn time and again. I also wonder if, speaking of religious references, that I sometimes blame God when things go especially wrong for me or for my loved ones. After all, if I have someone or some being to blame for life's difficulties, I have a place to vent my anger at what I see as injustice. Or as priest friend of mine was fond of saying, "Life sucks and then you die." Father Joe, in spite of his occupation, seems to be serious when he uses this phrase.

Sean's health is not the only recent time I have tapped into my religious doubts. For example, seeing my parents' deterioration toward the end of each of their respective lives prompted a similar reaction in me. Much earlier, my little brother died under mysterious circumstances when he was barely forty years old. While his death was ruled as the result of natural causes, I still have some doubts about the cause of his demise at such a young age.

It must be obvious by now that I still struggle with my religious beliefs. Perhaps, this interest in and struggle with religion is a pattern in my life to date. I take a little comfort in that I seem to have been not the only family member who has struggled with his faith. In my role as a family historian and story-teller, I have found examples of my ancestors' struggles with their faith.

One ancestral life that comes to mind when I say this about faith is Clovis I, King of the Franks, a tribe that predated, but is related to the French. Clovis was a pagan ruler of one branch of the Frankish people. He was married to Chlotilde, the daughter of King Chilperic II of Burgundy.

Chlotilde argued ceaselessly for Clovis to convert from his pagan ways to the Catholic faith, but he steadfastly refused. When Clovis agreed to have their first child, Ingomer baptized, the child soon died, perhaps even at the baptismal ceremony itself. Clovis was furious and would hear no more about Catholicism, yet he did not interfere with Chlotilde's own faith practices. Still, when Chlotilde insisted that their second child be baptized, Clovis reluctantly agreed (Scherman, 1987, p.111).

By 496, Clovis' future seemed ominous. From the beginning of his reign, Clovis' kingdom was surrounded by powerful and dangerous neighbors. Some of these enemies were even Franks, but still were enemies of Clovis' tribe, the Salian Franks. He feared greatly for his kingdom. The Allemans, a Germanic tribal confederation like the Franks, threatened not only the nearby Kingdom of Cologne under King Sigebert, but Clovis' kingdom as well. Allying himself with Sigebert, Clovis and Sigebert met the Allemans 24 miles southwest of Cologne in what would become modern Germany. The battle did not go well for Clovis and Sigebert. The allies were about to be defeated by their archenemy. The story goes that Clovis prayed to the Christian God, perhaps thinking of his own dear wife at the same time, asking for help against the enemy. As Clovis finished his prayer, the Allemans surprisingly turned and fled the scene. Clovis and Sigebert had won the day at the Battle of Tolbiac.

Clovis' prayer had included a bargain with God—victory for religious conversion. And quite a bargain it was. Clovis took his own sister and half of his 6000-man army into the Christian Church with him. Suddenly, even the Catholic clergy embraced him as their king. Remegius/Remy, the Bishop of Reims, had instructed Clovis in the Catholic faith. This conversion would have a lasting effect on European history. Following Clovis' baptism at Reims on Christmas Day 503, the alliance between French kings and the Catholic Church was firmly fixed (Scherman, 1987, p.114). Clovis had been instructed in the Catholic faith and was baptized by the bishop of Reims, Remigius. The bishop was later canonized as St. Remigius.

Clovis spent the last four years of his life fighting and successfully eliminating his Frankish peers on the outer reaches of his territory. To his credit, he was able to expand and then solidify his kingdom.

He presided over Austrasia in the east with its capital in Metz, Neustria with its capital in Paris, Burgundy in the southeast with its capital in Lyon, and Aquitaine, with its capital in Poitiers—a vast kingdom indeed (Cole, 1995).

But, although Clovis died a Christian, he had not led an exemplary life. His life was that of a brutal and wild Teutonic warrior. Because he died a practicing Catholic, writers like Gregory of Tours painted a glowing picture of Clovis. The truth though was that he started wars and skirmishes against his neighbors and murdered some of this own relatives (Cole, 1995). And although Clovis established new churches in his lands, he did so as penance--one new church for each murdered relative.

Clovis died in Paris in 511 AD/CE. He was buried in St. Peter and Paul Church, a facility that he and Chlotilde had funded and had built at the urging of St. Genevieve. The church was later re-named the Abbey of St. Genevieve (Scherman, 1987, p.133).

So, it would appear I am in good company when I examine my relationship with the Christian God. If Clovis I and others of my ancestry can struggle with their faith as they/we confront our troubles, then perhaps I am merely carrying on a family tradition.

Scene 2: The inevitable end: My parents depart

The deterioration of my parents, especially my father's, was a shock to me and to my siblings. For me, it had been a slowly-forming, reluctant realization that my parents, and certainly my father, were human and vulnerable. Again, this was difficult for me because I had to admit to myself that contrary to my childish hopes, my parents would not live forever.

As their oldest child, they had appointed me as their power-of-attorney. It now seemed time for me to help them make some decisions. In some ways, helping with these decisions meant an official end to my own childhood. In his poem, *The Rainbow*, the poet William Wordsworth said "The child is the father of the man." Although Wordsworth had a different meaning of the words when he wrote them, it seemed to me that I was now my parents' "father."

Ten years ago, I was not sure what to do about my parents' lives as they were rapidly aging, and obviously deteriorating. In some ways, they had been my life-long friends. Now my father was repeatedly falling and he was generally failing to look after himself. As for my mother, she was slowly losing her mind. She was showing signs of dementia.

I had loved my parents as even adult children often do. Yet for as much as the prior decade, they had begun to feel like my children. I felt responsible for their care and well-being. Yet, I still had a full time job teaching education and psychology at a college far from my home. My available parental care time was very limited.

Being responsible for my parents' lives was not easy for me. In fact, I felt conflicted. They wanted my help, yet I wished to remain their child. I felt forced to choose between being that child, and making parental-like decisions for them. While I had felt emotionally close to both my mother and my father, I had especially looked up to my father. Still, for decades I could see his shortcomings. I suppose though that knowing some of my own faults made it somewhat easier to overlook my father's.

How was I to continue to idolize my father, yet be largely responsible for his well-being and for my mother's? It is so difficult to be a grown-up, especially when there are difficult decisions to be made. What if I made the wrong decisions? What if I selected an inappropriate place for them to live? And they did need a place to live.

Simply put, they could no longer stay in their own home. Their house was a split level, which meant that they each needed to navigate several sets of stairs with their frail legs and distorted senses of balance. Besides, their home was falling apart—quite literally. Surviving on social security benefits only, they could do no repairs, no normal maintenance work. My father had difficulty breathing when he mowed his lawn with his riding mower, which often broke down anyway.

In the long Midwestern winter season, even shoveling snow caused him great discomfort. He would shovel a few square feet of the white stuff, only to need to take a break to catch his breath. Eventually, we discovered that he had a slow-growing lung cancer.

In some ways, my father had been one of my childhood heroes. He had played unaffiliated minor league baseball in Cleveland as a young man in the 1930s. He played outfield for Class A teams in front of crowds of 100,000 or more—baseball was a major draw in those days. The games were played at old Brookside Park on the west side of town. He even claimed to not only have batted against a future Hall of Famer, but that he singled against that pitcher. That pitcher was Bob (Rapid Robert) Feller.

To an impressionable, young and aspiring ball-player like me, I was in awe of that story. I even searched the archives of the local newspapers looking for his name in the box score of the games in which he played. Without an exact date of a specific game, the search proved to be futile.

I also heard stories of the time he spent in the United States Army as a drill instructor. Like the plot in some grainy old black and white movie, he said he had longed to go overseas to fight the Nazis, rather than train others to do so. He finally got his wish granted in late 1944. Arriving in France that same year, his unit, the Sixteenth Armored Division under the leadership of General George Patton, marched across France, Belgium, and Germany. Finally reaching Plzen, Czechoslovakia (now the Czech Republic), they were the first American troops to enter Plzen. German soldiers were still occupying parts of the town. To a child in love with history, like me, to hear him tell about chasing Nazis soldiers across the rooftops of Plzen was inspiring and even thrilling.

Yet, here he was, a nonagenarian who was often losing his balance, and who had increasingly poor health. He was slowly dying of lung cancer. And I, the former little boy, shy and unassuming, was left in charge of the management of his financial and medical affairs. Again, my misgivings cropped up--How could I take on responsibility for a baseball-playing, war hero's life? Something had to change in my own life, and in my way of thinking about myself. I was already a father, and a grandfather. I had a college teaching job, a wife, a newer car, but I still doubted my ability to effectively manage my parents' lives.

I won't go into much detail about the many decisions I made for them, but I somehow found the strength to partially let go of my childhood, and tend to my parents' issues. The way I did this was to let go of most of my remaining hero-worship, and my desire to remain childlike. Instead, I forced myself to make a series of key, but relatively minor decisions and judgments. As the participants in Alcoholics Anonymous say, "[Take it] one day at a time." I was developing a new and revised identity.

I did the things I did for my parents out of duty, out of obligation, but also out genuine concern for their well-being. I took baby steps in my efforts to help keep them as comfortable as I could in the final months and years of their lives.

Still, I hesitated and I trembled with fear, dread, and longing when my father finally died on February 6, 2011. He died as he had lived, in a grandiose, larger than life final act of the play that was his life. In an assisted-living environment in a private home in a fine suburban Cleveland neighborhood, he held court. Present were his children, his grandchildren, some of his great-grandchildren, and a few friends who had stopped to say good-bye.

In desperation, I held my father's hand. Then I gave him one final kiss on his face. I cried out, "I'm not ready for you to go!" Suddenly and to my great surprise, he responded, "I'll stay!" I burst into tears when he said he would wait. But, his now-frail body almost seemed as if his spirit, his life force was departing this world. Three hours later, he was gone. The man I thought was invincible was now gone forever. And I had had the honor, the privilege of seeing him out the door, and on his way. *Requiescat in pace,* Papa! Who needs to watch television soap operas when one's own life can be such a melodrama?

My mother would die barely a year after my father. Following my parents' deaths in the second decade of the twenty-first century—they were both well into their nineties--I was still not ready for their deaths. Picking out their caskets at their preferred funeral home was a painful and difficult chore for me. Following each of their deaths, I spent day after day in tears—while "shopping" at the funeral home, at the wake, at the funeral Mass, at the cemetery, then when the requisite death-connected events were over, I cried some more at home. What I missed most was being able to hear their stories about their respective childhoods. There would be no more story-telling unless it came from me, and would anyone be there to hear these tales?

As a writer, I miss being able to share with my parents the stories about our newly-discovered ancestors. What a shame they missed hearing about my mother's various grandparents and her multiple times great-grandparents. To share an exciting story with those I love is one of the joys of my adult life. Perhaps, in some future lifetime, my parents and I could sit around a campfire on a starlit summer night, while I regale them with tales of long, long ago. What a delightful fantasy! And if a campfire were not available for story-time, how about curling up in a booth at a fine little White Castle® restaurant?

I can hear the opening conversation now:

"Mom? Dad? Wait 'til tell you this one—ya' just gotta' hear it!"

In my fantasy, they would respond in unison, "OK, son. Let's have it. Let's have your story of those relatives long gone." They would then collectively add, "Let's have another one of your wonderful tales." I would smile broadly, and begin again with yet another story of the ancients, our ancient ones.

Scene 3: Telling tales out of school

I have often wondered what has driven me to become the family story-teller. It seems to me that at least five factors were at work in my journey from the shy boy who took solace in quiet reading of non-fiction to the adult who first researched then wrote biographies of the family members I discovered.

First, as the oldest child and the oldest grandchild of my family of origin, I simply had (and still have) more access to family stories and family history than did my siblings and cousins. Recently, I took inventory of the names and descriptions of as many of the members of my family of origin and my extended family as I could recall. In all, I identified 33 aunts, uncles, cousins, and others that I knew personally and of whom I had memories. As an educated guess, I believe that my siblings and/or cousins might remember only about twenty of these relatives.

Second, I have been interested in history since my early childhood. Although I majored in history in undergraduate college training, I was often bored with the abstractness of the subject. It was the biographies of individuals that caught and kept my interest. Tracking down family members through first- hand research was so different than traditional history classes were, and not the least abstract to me! I could examine the lives of real people using the time period of their lives as background to make these characters come to life.

Third, I had retired from teaching several years ago. Suddenly, I had a lot of free time to do what I wanted. I still worried about making financial ends meet, but Sheila kindly agreed to let me write to my heart's content, while she continued to work a regular job (if a

50-60 hour work week can be considered "regular"). Again, thank you, my dear.

While I thoroughly enjoyed teaching for the first 25 years of my career, it was a great relief to free up my time to get my life together. What I mean by "getting my life together" is that for the first time since childhood, I had time to *think* without the pressure of performing on the job. There was now no one to give me an annual review, no one to tell me how much of a raise I would be getting, and no one to tell me what I needed to improve upon in my work. What a godsend!

Yet, I did not know at the time of my retirement that I would become a writer—not consciously anyway. I knew that I enjoyed researching my family's history and gathering tales from my family's lore, but as for putting my research results into book form, I had no plans for doing that. Because I had taught college for three decades, publishing was part of the expectations of the job. Yet, I wrote only the bare minimum that I needed to get by in my annual work evaluations.

And even then, I often did not write what I had enthusiastic interest in writing about, but rather I wrote what would get me through the evaluations. "See, boss—I did do some publishing since last year's evaluation." Granted, this was not very rewarding or even very honest behavior on my part.

The fourth factor that has spurred me on to oral storytelling and to writing is that I feared losing thirty years of research. Inspecting the many piles of photocopied and original documents I had gathered over the decades, I wondered what would happen to my mountainous pile of papers at my death. My parents' demise gave me a rather sudden realization that I would not live forever! After all, now that they were gone, my generation was next in line to check out of this world.

As a man who had just turned seventy years of age, I began to fantasize about the end of my own life. I could imagine my loved ones going through the dozens of boxes and tens of thousands of pages of family history documents I had left behind at my demise. I had already lost to death my brother, numerous aunts, uncles, and cousins, and most recently my parents. Getting older provides all of us with such losses. Still, we seldom take the time to mull over our own fate.

What would others do with these materials? Organize them into usable stacks? Write a book or article using the data I had collected? Give them away in a completely unorganized state to some library? I know what I would have done.

Initially, I would have diligently gone through the material, trying to make sense of what I was seeing. I would have contacted other relatives—siblings, cousins, perhaps elderly aunts or uncles as well. "Will you help me go through these boxes of materials? Will you help me organize this 'stuff'? Do you want this material?"

And in the end, I would have given up. I would have judged myself disloyal and would likely have felt guilty. But, after all was said and done, I believe I would have pitched the entire batch of "stuff" into the nearest dumpster. What a wasteful act destroying this material would have been! What a loss to current and future generations.

So there it was. Boxes and boxes and reams and reams of material about my ancient and more recent family. And there would almost certainly be no one to do anything constructive with this plethora of data. No one except for me! Could I do it—could I organize these materials into useful batches? Better still, could I take the organized "stuff" and put it into a readable format—one that would tell my family and the rest of the world (if they chose to do the reading) who my family was and what we (our ancestors and the living) had contributed to life on earth? How's that for grandiose questions and statements?

The fifth and final factor that led me to become the family storyteller was my desire to gain a taste of immortality. After all, my body would someday stop functioning, and I would become just a memory to those I left behind. But, a book could last forever in one form or another. A book, those objects of knowledge that I had cherished since I first learned to read, could become my earthly salvation.

Keeping all of these factors in mind, I began to take responsibility for not only organizing thirty years' worth of family story-gathering, but I put pen to paper, and wrote not one, but two collections of family stories. It was very difficult work. I must admit that conducting the research and organizing data collection was the easy part. I found the actual writing of these two books to be grueling and tedious work. I hope that I have not scandalized any budding authors by 'fessing up to the difficulties of writing, but I believe a memoir is nothing if it is not an honest account of one's experiences. And one final thought—Please buy and read my books!

Scene 4: Milestones

As a septuagenarian, I can tell you that getting to be part of the older generation is not much fun. When I awaken in the morning, I am stiff and slow to move about the room. Looking in the mirror as I shave or brush my teeth, I am at times surprised at the physical traits of the old person looking back at me. In short, I am watching myself grow old!

And if the obvious physical changes in appearance were not enough, there is the fact that my vision is failing and my hearing is a victim of the Powers-Underwood genetic defect—loss of hearing especially in my right ear. Added to this list is the handful of daily medications I take to compensate for an imperfect body. Such revelations could make for a steady stream of negative thoughts.

However, one of the absolute joys of aging is to look back on one's actual accomplishments. I have come to think of these accomplishments as *milestones*. Literally, a milestone is a roadside marker that shows the distance left before arrival at a particular destination. Yet for me, I see a milestone as a special moment when I feel the need to reflect on my life. That moment usually follows some accomplishment or significant event.

When I try to recall those special moments that have served as road signs that pointed me in new directions, I remember a handful of these unique times. At least sixteen of these events seem significant, although all were not positive.

Still, every marker forced me to take stock of my life, reflecting on and analyzing them in detail. Let me forewarn you here. The list of milestones that follows reads like some staid and stale employment resume. For example, I:

Graduated from high school in a college preparatory track
Graduated from undergraduate college with a major in history
Married for the first time at age 23
Personally witnessed the birth of my two biological children
Was accepted into the Peace Corps/VISTA and completed my tour of duty
Was divorced at the age of 39
Was selected to the Urban Teacher Corps at the University of Pittsburgh
Obtained a license to teach comprehensive social studies
Earned licensure as a professional clinical counselor
Was offered and accepted a college teaching job at age 26
Met and married my second wife
Experienced the death of my much-younger brother
Completed an original, published research project on broken hearts
Earned a doctorate in psychology
Experienced the deaths of my parents within 13 months of each other
Wrote and published two non-fiction books about my ancient ancestors

When I look at these milestones and compare these with the picture I had of myself at ages 5-20, I feel somewhat shocked. My life changed dramatically after my early twenties. In both childhood and adolescence I saw myself as a shy, rather backward person who had relatively few advantages in life at the time. Bashfulness, a mediocre self-image, poverty, parental alcoholism, and hunger were my frequent companions. I had very few healthy role models, and even less mentoring and guidance. I think it is safe to say, I did not have the most supportive environment in which to thrive during those early years. Not only was my environment lacking, my personality was not conducive to creating a "success" story.

    I suppose that this last statement is true for many people—one's early years may say little about successes and failures in later life. Hearing these words gives me hope for my own future, but especially for my children and grandchildren, and generations of Powers and Chylinski descendants in the future.

Scene 5: The future not yet written

Speaking of the *future,* I am well aware that there may not be all that much of that commodity left to me. In short, I might have only a few years remaining in my life. Tomorrow is not promised to any of us, and those of us who are up there in years have even more reason to feel pessimistic about our time going forward!

In contrast to my attitude when I was in my teens, twenties, and thirties, I find myself being cautious and conservative about how I spend my days. I have asked myself questions such as, "Where do I want to travel next?" And, "How many more big trips do I have left in me?" By big trips I mean airline flights of more than five or six hours. When I was young, time seemed to stretch forward endlessly. Now, every moment takes on a new urgency. Truthfully, extensive travel, while still fascinating, flat-out tires me. So, I ask myself, "Is this how I intend to spend the balance of my precious time?"

That having been said, I am now planning to take a final, single, long-distance trip to Australia and New Zealand next year. Although I celebrated my thirtieth wedding anniversary this year, it is during my 32nd year of marriage to Sheila that we will make this journey across the Pacific Ocean to the land down under. While I am fascinated by these far-away and in my mind, exotic countries of the Pacific, I am also well aware that my father, an avid reader of the magazine *National Geographic,* wanted to make a similar trip.

I cannot live his life for him, and even if I had the ability to do that, he is now deceased. So there is a certain poetic justice in traveling this route in his stead. I am now seeking suggestions from others, including my six remaining siblings, about what items that belonged to my father I might take with me, leaving these items there as a kind of vicarious journey for my father. Any thoughts about what items I might leave?

Other ways I hope to spend my limited supply of years include the following:

Edit and publish a set of 105 letters that my parents exchanged with each other during WWII.

Re-write and publish as a second edition my first book, *Saints, Sinners, Scoundrels, and Some Ordinary People*. I am dissatisfied with the handful of errors in this 300-plus page volume.

Settle myself on my religious beliefs—I subscribe to an online web site, www.closertotruth.com that discusses such matters in general.

Buy a tombstone for my paternal grandfather, Wladislaw Chylinski. Currently grandpa lies in an unmarked grave in Calvary Cemetery in Cleveland, Ohio. His gravesite is in an isolated area of the cemetery, where perhaps I am the only person on earth who knows exactly where he is buried. Wladislaw's survivors simply had no money during the latter part of the Great Depression to purchase a grave marker for him. While his consort, my paternal grandmother, also lies in an unmarked grave, Grandpa Chylinski has waited the longest to be recognized—he died in 1940, fully 78 years ago. He is a man I never knew, but I am prepared to give this gift to him.

Continue my research on the Powers, Underwood, and Chylinski families. I am not likely to publish any more books about members of these families, but finding dead people makes me happy. It is thrilling to me to discover previously-unknown relatives.

Continue to serve as the editor of the *Hudson Green*, the official newsletter of the Hudson Genealogical Study Group, an arm of the Hudson (Ohio) Library and Historical Society. To date, I have published five or six articles in this publication. And this was *before* I volunteered to take on the editing task. With my new-found power, just imagine how many articles I can publish in the future!

Buy a puppy, probably a Shih Tzu to replace my 16-year-old friend, Mattie, who died in January 2017. Nearly blind, disoriented, and incontinent, we had her euthanized at the offices of our longtime veterinarian.

Continue to run and exercise at my local health center, if only to keep my wife from pestering me with her favorite cheer, "Use it or lose it, buddy!" In fairness to Sheila, I do feel better after I have exercised—that is, after many days have passed, and I have recovered from my physical ordeal.

Attend the wakes and funerals of friends and relatives. As I age, more and more of my associates are disappearing permanently. Up to this time in my life, I have steadfastly avoided attending such events unless I felt obligated to do so. These obligational (is there such a word?) forays into the ways of death have included the wakes of not only my parents and grandparents, but also those of numerous aunts, uncles, cousins, and of course that of my younger brother. *Requiescat in pace*, my friends.

Visit with all eight of my grandchildren as their time and mine allow. Most live within 50 miles of my home. Staying in touch with my Florida-based grandsons will be a bit more difficult. Jacksonville is a troublesome place to reach, even when I am in already in the state of Florida. Few flights head to that destination, and it is a 900-mile drive from my northern house, and a 350-mile drive from my Florida home.

Occasionally buy cars for the sole purpose of re-selling them at a small profit. This is a "hobby" I honed while watching my maternal grandfather William Henry Powers (1887-1966) operate. Fortunately for Papaw, the Hudsons, Packards, and the odd Chevrolets or Fords he discovered never cost him more than $100 per vehicle. Inflation would have done in Grandpa, as I cannot find a decent vehicle to resell for less than $3000.00.

Spend all or nearly all of each winter in some warm climate. My wife still works full-time and year-round. This puts a damper on my dream of escaping Ohio winters entirely. Staying in the warmth alone while she continues to labor in the fields is simply more than I believe I can tolerate. I have high hopes for her to take an early retirement thus freeing us both up for a long stay in some anti-winter locale.

Die. By this, I don't mean that I am actually looking forward to death. It's just that I cannot avoid it. At the risk of sounding more pedantic than usual, the existential fact of life is that each of us must exit this world. And that includes me. I would like to prepare in some way for my inevitable demise. How to do that remains to be seen.

With a bit of gallows humor, I remember a joke about two gentlemen having a discussion on this very topic. They are wondering if there is baseball played in the afterlife. They promise each other that the first one to die will find some way to notify the other whether baseball exists after death. One week later, one of the friends dies. Shortly after, the living friend recognizes a voice coming out of the clouds. It is his deceased friend's words that he hears. "Joe, I have some good news and some bad news. The good news: There *is* baseball in the afterlife. The bad news is that you are pitching on Friday."

While I may be too decrepit to play baseball now or in the afterlife, my hope is that at least I can watch a season or two of games à la the sports movie, *Field of Dreams*. In that Hollywood film, Kevin Costner (as the character Ray Kinsella) watches baseball games that feature long since dead major league stars of the sport.

Although I am still relatively healthy and very active, I can hear the roll of thunder in the distance that W.H. Auden mentioned in his poem *Marginalia*. I always did like the sounds of summer thunderstorms!

Death is the roll
of distant thunder at a picnic.

Reflecting on My Search for Identity

Introduction

It seems to me that deciding on one's identity is a terribly complicated process. For one thing, there seems to be an array of definitions for the term, *identity*, at least in academic circles. Sometimes, the concept is given alternative names such as *sense of self* and *narrative identity*. Essentially the definitions for each of these terms appear virtually the same.

For example, the social psychologist Don McAdams (2001) says that a *narrative identity* is created when "individuals form an identity by integrating their life experiences into an internalized, evolving story of the self that provides the individual with a sense of unity and purpose in life (p.1)." Further, McAdams says that this life narrative integrates an individual's reconstructed past, with his/her perceived present, and imagined future. https://en.wikipedia.org/wiki/Narrative_Identity Retrieved 1/17/2018.

Later, McAdams (2008) defined *narrative identity* as "an internalized and evolving story of the self that reconstructs the past and anticipates the future in such a way as to provide a person's life with some degree of unity, meaning, and purpose over time (p.1)." http://nobaaproject.com/modules/self-and-identity Retrieved 1/17/2018.

The psychological researcher and author Parker J. Palmer (2008) says that *identity* is ever-evolving, and is influenced by "… [our] loved ones, those we cared for, people who have harmed us and people we have harmed, the deeds done (good and ill) to self and others, experiences lived, and choices made [which] come together to form who we are at this moment (p.1)." https://en.wikipedia.org/wiki/Identity_formation Retrieved 12/20/2017.

Additionally, there appear to be several distinct and separate facets to a person's identity (including my own) rather than being a single, simple, one-dimensional concept. According to Palmer (2008), there are genetic, cultural, professional, ethnic, national, religious, and gender aspects to this phenomenon. https://en.wikipedia.org/wiki/Identity_formation Retrieved 11/20/2017.

And in a tutorial sponsored by the Brain Injury Association of New York State, we hear that sense of self or personal identity includes for most people a number of important ways of thinking about themselves that are significant enough to be considered *multiple senses of self* [italics are mine]. [Further]... self-identities, especially those of young people, are dynamic or in flux. http://www.projectlearnet.org/TUTORIAL/SENSE_OF_SELF_PERSONAL_IDENTITY.HTML Retrieved 3/14/2018.

In my own not-so-humble opinion, my *search for identity* has been strongly influenced by six factors: 1) the judgments and opinions of significant others, especially in childhood and adolescence, 2) my accomplishments, 3) experimentation, i.e. trying on various roles and identities in assorted areas, e.g. sports, academics, interpersonal relationships, and so forth, 4) my personality, 5) other miscellaneous data, e.g. genealogical or biological/DNA discoveries, and 6) losses, gains, and changes in my health, financial, relationship and/or career statuses. Of course, these events—losses, gains, and various life changes happen to everyone. It seems obvious that this sixth factor hints at the tentative and somewhat fragile nature of identity. The formation of my identity has been multifaceted and is an ongoing process that can and probably will last for the balance of my lifetime.

As I reflect on the sources that helped me create my identity, it appears that researchers Palmer and McAdams are correct in that there are at the very least several areas of identity, and perhaps there are even a handful of separate kinds of identity rather than a single, personal identity. Collectively, these separate kinds of identity may combine to form my core identity. For example, there is:

- The relationship me
- The academic me
- The religious me
- The professional, job-centered me
- The personality me, a largely inherited phenomenon

- The physical, athletic me
- The ethnic me
- The cultural me
- The gender me
- The national me
- The genetic me

When I first began my memoir/life narrative, I set out two tasks for myself. One was to decide who I was today, knowing as I did, that at the very least both my life experiences and the results of my family research could have altered my earlier view of myself. In a second task in my search for my identity, I thought I might also be able to discover why I chose to become the family story-teller in the first place.

In this concluding section of my memoir, I intend to:

- Examine some themes in my life experiences and their influence on my identity
- Analyze my personality and its relationship to my identity search
- Discuss some of my genealogical findings and see how they may affect my sense of identity
- Examine DNA test results for my parents and myself
- Verify that we are all Africans and that we are all cousins
- Share some final thoughts on my search for identity

Themes in my life experiences and their role in my search for identity

At first glance, my life experiences seem to me to be a hodgepodge of isolated incidents. Still, when I examine them more closely, some of these experiences do have common themes.

One theme that repeats itself is *helplessness*. In Act One, Childhood, there are at least four instances when I felt helpless—at a loss about what to do to feel safe or to extricate myself from some difficult situation. Saying this, I can recall feeling like a helium-filled balloon, drifting at the mercy of the winds during some of my childhood. Perhaps this feeling is every child's fate as he/she journeys from a state of dependence and weakness to one of strength and mastery. I just know I did not like feeling this way. Two other themes appear in my childhood experiences—success in school, at times by "stretching", that is behaving in ways outside my comfort zone. Another significant theme is my love of family. This has been a repetitive theme throughout this memoir and my life.

These two themes—success in school and love of family--may have even paved the way for a few positive events in my life. Yet, feeling a strong need for and love of family may have also set me on a path to hurt in my first marriage. For example, being tightly bound to my spouse and children on such an emotional level made it all the more difficult to withstand the breakup when that marriage ended in the 1980s.

In Act Two, Adolescence, I can identify such themes as immature people skills and loneliness, which was the price that I paid for my innate shyness. I often did not have my voice heard because I failed to speak up allowing it to be heard. Also, there were early signs of the adventurous me. One adventure was a physical and potentially dangerous one—the gun battle in the gully. Still, though my people skills were poorly developed, I also showed signs of an interest in other people by maintaining a group of supportive friends in childhood—fellow adventurers. Finally in my interactions with Sister Margaret Thomas, I found a healthy role model. More importantly, I began to see in my relationship with Sister Margaret the possibility that a family could be chosen, not just inherited. What a revelation that became as I later reflected on my relationship with this nun!

In my early adulthood tales (Act Three), I could see another example of my immature people skills in my encounter with Karen Krandahl. In not speaking out to her in defense of my faith, I again failed to have my voice heard. Thinking back on that event, it seems that her approval was more important to me than was defending my beliefs. Still, in my early adulthood I began to experiment with love, reaching out to Karla with a degree of assertiveness I had seldom shown early earlier. Again, the adventurer theme reared its head when I boarded that sailboat only to be met by an Atlantic storm.

In another early adulthood story involving the sea, I dared to start a new life with my newly-added wife by moving overseas. Joining the domestic Peace Corps, I seemed to have had a belief that I could handle not only the adjustment of a life in a foreign land, but also the adjustment to life as a newlywed. Or perhaps I was simply too young and inexperienced to understand how difficult my adjustment to overseas life and to marriage would be.

Another adventure awaited me around the next corner. But this time it was an emotional one. Writing love letters during Marriage Encounter "dialogues" as our love-letter discussions were called forced me to explore my sense of self in way I had never before experienced. I was asked to dwell on my purpose in life, and then to write about this purpose. Even more difficult was that I shared my answers verbally with my wife. I shed many tears then.

Marriage Encounter required that I reflect on this and on other soul-searching questions. It took a certain amount of courage to explore the depth of my own values and beliefs. I accepted this challenge, and I shared my answers to these questions with my wife and life's partner (so I thought) in a way I could not have imagined earlier. What I did not readily realize was that by going deeper into my psyche and sharing what I did with another human being was dangerous behavior, not physically in a, "Let's brave the fury of the seas" kind of way, but in an adventure that required me to plumb the depths of my emotional and values-laden self. It felt to me like I was opening myself to a vulnerability I had never before known.

I truly began to know myself thanks to the M.E. experience. About this same time, I listened to and took the advice of my first mother-in-law. At her suggestion, I embarked on a career in teaching that would become my life's work for nearly four decades. Interestingly, what I chose to teach—education and psychology—I see now as an extension of those risky love letters during the years in Marriage Encounter. Both of those fields seemed to require the educator to know himself/herself and to give to others. So becoming a teacher may also have helped me to understand myself a bit better. Teaching certainly allowed me to grow and to serve as a role model to others. In his 2018 article, *The Heart of a Teacher*, Parker Palmer seems to agree with that analysis. Parker says:

Teaching holds a mirror to the soul, [and] if I am willing to look in that mirror, and not run from what I see, I have a chance to gain self-knowledge—and knowing myself is a s crucial to good teaching as knowing my students and my subject (p.1). Face to face with my students, only one resource is at my immediate command: my identity, my self-hood, my sense of this "I" who teaches—without which I have no sense of the "Thou" that learns (p.2).

Parker continues: [and] by identity, I mean an evolving nexus where all the forces that constitute my life converge in the mystery of self: my genetic makeup, the nature of the man and woman who gave me life, the culture in which I was raised, people who sustained me and people who have done me harm, the good and ill I have done to others, and to myself, the experience of love and suffering—and much, much more. In the midst of that complex field, identity is a moving intersection of the inner and outer forces that make me who I am, converging in the irreducible mystery of being human (p.4).

He goes on to declare: those are my definitions—but try as I may to refine them, they always come out too pat. *Identity and integrity can never be fully named or known by anyone, including the person who bears them. They constitute familiar strangeness we take with us to the grave, elusive realities that can be caught only occasionally out of the corner of the eye (p.4).*[italics are mine].

Parker concludes that: we become teachers for reasons of the heart, animated by a passion for some subject and for helping people to learn (p.6).

In middle age (Act Four), I realized for the first time that by loving Karla, I risked getting emotionally hurt. To hear that someone loved me like a brother, someone who I loved as a life-long partner, was almost more than I could bear. The lesson I learned about the dangers of mature love appeared at least three times during my middle years. Yet, "keeping it shallow" by engaging in callous, careless sexual behavior with people I scarcely knew was not the answer to protecting myself from pain.

Instead, my thoughtless behavior was just a salve that briefly nourished a wound, making it feel a bit better for a time. Now, I understand that wounds must heal from the inside outward. So the salve of my profligate behavior was only a temporary expediency. The wound remains to this day, no longer festering, but aching dully like the way a broken bone aches on a damp, dreary, and dull rainy day—an arthritis of the soul that I carry with me to this day.

Relationships, I learned, do not necessarily end when they appear to die. Feelings go on as do memories of earlier times. We carry with us that which we cannot seem to forget. In his play, *I Never Sang For My Father*, Robert Anderson reminded us that "Death ends a life, not a relationship, which struggles on the minds of the survivors toward some resolution which it can never find." Anderson knew what he was talking about. I believe he was also alluding to not just the "big death" that we and our loved ones experience, but the hundreds of "little deaths" we suffer—divorce, job loss, loss of our youth, and more.

My middle years also provided more excitement, more adventures. Some adventures were of the heart, like learning to risk again. Emotional risk-taking led me to love again. Other adventures were the physical-type, flying to far-away places, meeting strange and wonderful people, demonstrating my adult ability to confront unique, unfamiliar, and potentially dangerous situations.

Still, I re-experienced the theme of hurt I feel when others disapprove of me. In the case of the Catholic college at which I taught, I fear that there was irreparable damage done there to my religious beliefs. I cannot explain how or why I now feel more doubts about the nature of God—I am still a believer, but the God I see now is not the all-loving, all-kind being I experienced as a child.

And while I am not sure of the exact connection between my negative experiences with the Fortevrists and my current "doubting-Thomas" attitude toward my religious beliefs, there does seem to be a connection. This is not to blame anyone in particular, but I keep recalling what I perceived as the negative judgments that several school administrators made about the quality of my faith. Certainly, this is an unpleasant memory from my middle adulthood.

In my dotage, Act Five, I am reminded still again that love can hurt. No matter if the good-bye is said to a former spouse or if the *adios* is for the departure of parents, the pain is all too familiar. How interesting the word *adios* is. In its common use, the word simply means good-bye or farewell. But, of course in the literal translation in the Spanish language the word means "until God." I would rejoice to see my parents again, with or without God's presence. Although I have said goodbye to each of my parents, I still feel a dull ache when I think of them, especially on holidays and on their birthdays.

Once again, I am reminded of a scene from the motion picture, *Field of Dreams*, when the hero, Ray Kinsella meets his deceased father on the baseball field that Ray has built. He says to his father, "Would you like to have a catch?" Oh, for one more opportunity to play catch with a baseball with my father.

Loss seems nothing new or out-of-the-ordinary to me. As the family story-teller, I've seen hundreds of examples of loss in the lives of my ancestors, many of which qualify as tragic—the death of a child, the violent death of the family bread-winner, the passing of a woman in childbirth. Still, in my old age I am reminded of the importance of family. While each family has a beginning and an inevitable end, at least its existence and its contributions can be recorded in writing. Love (and its demise) may hurt, but its memory might be helped to live on through story-telling. Love's sweet aroma might continue to drift through the air like the scent of flowering trees in the springtime.

Another theme I've identified in my later life experiences is that merely writing this life narrative is a risk. What if I hear negative feedback on this book? After all, it is not a novel, not science fiction, it is my life—a recounting of my years on earth. While my memoir is not me, criticism of it will likely still hurt. On a more positive note, it seems to me that my memoir is a kind of *redemptive narrative*. I do feel pleased with that thought of redemption.

A redemptive narrative can take more than one form. McAdams (2013) says that a person might travel "from suffering to an enhanced status or state, while scripting the development of a chosen protagonist who journeys forth into a dangerous and unredeemed world" (p. 10), like some Hollywood movie character. As wholesome as that description might sound, I can assure you that my life story made into a movie would not be "G-rated."

McAdams further notes in his 1997 research project conducted with his co-authors Diamond, de St. Aubin, &Mansfield, "American adults who enjoy high levels of mental health and civic engagement tend to construct their lives as *narratives of redemption* [italics are mine], tracking the move from sin to salvation, rags to riches, oppression to liberation, or sickness/abuse to health/recovery (in McAdams, 2013, p. 10)." My thanks go to McAdams for making me look mentally healthy. Still, being mentally healthy does not preclude pain from losses or from the simple passage of precious time.

In my own case, I did journey from great poverty in a rat-infested house in the inner city of Cleveland, with a non-assertive mother and an alcoholic father, to a life of relative ease and some educational and financial success. For that I am grateful and not a little proud.

The final theme I discovered in Act Five, Old Age, is that as the retired movie star and pop singer, Doris Day sang, *"Que sera sera*, the future's not ours to see." In fact, managing my future is a matter of *managing maybes*. I hope for the best, I plan, I value, I guide myself, but I am left to direct what merely could be and what might be.

After analyzing the themes I discovered in my life experiences, I am still left with the question, "Who Am I?" There are other significant influences on my search for my identity. These include my personality traits, the results of my genealogical research, DNA test results of my parents and myself, and the idea that all humans alive today are descended from Africans (or are still African), plus the research of geneticists who found that we are all at least 50th cousins. I want to look now at each of these influences.

My personality and the search for identity:

When I reflect on the events in my life, I can see clear examples of my personality traits surfacing. There are many definitions for personality and nearly as many theories of this concept. But, the most widely accepted theory is what McCrae and Costa (1992) call the *Big Five Personality Traits* theory. It is sometimes referred to simply as the *Five Factor Model (FFM)*.

Very briefly, this model discusses five general dimensions used by psychologists and others to describe human personality. The acronyms OCEAN or CANOE represent each factor in the theory. The letters stand for (in the OCEAN acronym) openness, conscientiousness, extraversion, agreeableness, and neuroticism. Without going into great depth here, one definition of personality is "individual differences in characteristic patterns of thinking, feeling, and behaving" (American Psychological Association, 2017).

The trait of openness to experience refers to a person's willingness to try doing new things, opening one-self to being vulnerable, and willingness to think outside the box. The second trait, conscientiousness, is the tendency to control one's impulses, and to engage in socially-acceptable behavior, while often performing goal-directed behavior. The third trait, extraversion, represents the desire and ability to draw energy from social interactions, while an introverted person draws energy from solitude. Introverted people get tired of social interaction rather quickly, and look for some quiet space to replenish their supply of energy. https://positivepsychologyprogram.com/big-five-personality-theory/ Retrieved 4/23/2018.

The final two elements of the Big Five theory are agreeableness and neuroticism. How well does and individual get along with other people? That is the question asked about a person's agreeableness personality factor. Those high in this trait generally act kindly, and they tend to be liked and respected. They are sensitive to the needs of others. Finally, neuroticism has to do, not with any type of neurosis or mental illness, but rather it refers to how comfortable a person is with himself/herself. Further, those people high in neuroticism tend to be overly sensitive, anxious, nervous, timid, fearful, and typically are low in self-esteem. https://positivepsychologyprogram.com/big-five-personality-theory/ Retrieved 4/23/2018. Those low in neuroticism are not overly sensitive, and they tend to be less anxious, nervous, and fearful than their counterparts.

All five of McCrae's and Costa's personality trait dichotomies can be placed on continua. An individual's level of a particular trait might be at one of the extreme ends of the trait or a trait might appear somewhere near the middle. In other words, shy people do not all have exactly the same amount of shyness, nor are those who carry the disagreeableness trait necessarily extreme in their display of that trait, and so forth.

According to Lahey (2009), individuals vary dramatically on the neuroticism scale, ranging from "frequent and intense emotional reactions to minor challenges to little emotional reaction even in the face of significant difficulties p. 1)." Those high in neuroticism are often sensitive to the criticism of others and are self-critical as well. Further, those who score high on this scale may also feel personally inadequate. I do confess to being very self-critical and to being sensitive to criticism from others. Lahey also notes that this trait of neuroticism typically diminishes in adulthood, and in my case, I can testify that this has been true for me. For what it is worth, females have significantly higher scores on average than do males on this scale.

But, all of these details do not explain where my personality fits into this theory or how my personality has affected my sense of identity. Based on the descriptions of McCrae and Costa of the five sets of personality dichotomies, I created a table (see below) that demonstrates where I believe I stand on each dichotomous scale.

Extraversion_____X_____ Introversion
Emotional Stability_____X_____ Neuroticism
Agreeableness___X_____ Disagreeableness
Conscientiousness___X_____Nonconscientiousness
Openness to experience___X_____ Conventionality

Summarizing, I see myself as introverted on the extraversion-introversion continuum, tending toward neuroticism on the emotional stability scale, and generally agreeable, conscientious and open to experiences on those scales. Most of these traits are inheritable, so I can thank my parents and to some degree, my four grandparents for their contributions to my personality.

A fascinating study was conducted by the University of Minnesota on the inheritability of personality traits in the 1970's. Hundreds of pairs of twins were brought together for six days of testing that included testing of blood, brain waves, allergies, and intelligence. Among the separately-reared twins, there were forty-four pairs of identical twins and twenty-one pairs of fraternal twins. Many of the twins were raised apart beginning shortly after birth, and some even met for the first time during the study.

Briefly, the researchers found that for the traits that were studied, heredity was responsible for more than half of all the traits discovered. Of course, this also means that a little less than half of the traits could be accounted for by family environment or by life experiences. Further, of the eleven personality traits examined, the differences between hereditary and environmental influences were significantly smaller than the scientists anticipated.

Among the traits most strongly influenced by heredity were leadership and obedience to authority or traditionalism. Other traits that were significantly influenced by heredity were vulnerability to stress (and its opposite, resistance to stress), fearfulness to risk-taking, and alienation, and surprisingly, a tendency to engage in rapt experiences, such as throwing oneself into the music at a concert. Another way to describe vulnerability to stress is the Costa and

McCrae term, *neuroticism*. Those twins high in neuroticism tended to be jumpy, easily irritated, and fairly dissatisfied with themselves. The need to achieve also appeared to be strongly influenced by genetics, yet life experiences seemed to be even more influential in the desire to achieve. The same lower genetic influence was true for impulsiveness and its opposite, caution. http://www.nytimes.com/1986/12/02/science/major-personality-study-finds-that-traits-are-mostly-inherited.htm Retrieved 2/5/2018.

Still, I have made some adjustments in my behaviors over time. These changes have enabled me to reach out to others and to make my voice heard on many occasions. In fact, some of the milestones I have reached would not have been possible if not for my "acting as if" I was confident and had the requisite skills to be successful. What comes to mind here are the dozen or so speeches I have made, and the very fact that I have willed myself to be the center of attention in the many hundreds of college classes I have taught. One particularly poignant moment I recall from my teaching days took place at the end of a term. A student who I did not know especially well said to me, "I don't think of you as a teacher. I think of you as a friend who knows a lot." I cherish that student's words to this day, and I feel proud of my willingness to extend myself beyond my "natural" comfort zone.

Genealogical findings and my search for identity

The jury is still debating about whether genealogy is relevant in helping people discover their identity. For example, Nathan H. Lents (2018) asked this question: "What does it say that Barack Obama and Dick Cheney are distant relatives sharing an ancestor [Mareen Duvall, a French Huguenot who arrived in British Maryland in 1650] more than 400 years ago: If you ask me, I say, it means almost nothing. Until he entered *politics* [Lents' italics], the life of Barack Obama could not have been more different than that of Dick Cheney" (p.1). Here, Lents' mathematics skills show a definite shortcoming. As of today, Duvall came to the English colony 368 years ago, not 400 plus years.
https://www.psychologytoday.com/us/blog/beastlybehavior/201801/the-meaning-and-meaninglessness-genealogy Retrieved3/19/2018.

Later, in the article entitled *The Meaning and Meaninglessness of Genealogy*, Lents (2018, p.4) questions those people who value genealogical research as a tool for altering identity, "If you found out that... a French aristocrat had seduced or even raped your great-grandmother, how would that change your self-identity? I sure hope it wouldn't change it at all. The culture in which we are raised shapes us as much as our parents do."

Paradoxically though, in that same *Psychology Today* article, Lents admits to prominently displaying photographs of his distant ancestors in his bedroom, and will recount stories of the lives of these long-gone blood relatives if asked. It seems that Lents wants it both ways—"I don't care who my ancestors were. But while you are in my house take a look at these photos of my forebears." At best, it appears to me that Lents is ambivalent about the usefulness of family research and its influence on identity, as he says he has a "... wall of ancestors that I've never met, but whose story I tell" (p.5).

On the other hand, Russell Baker, that intrepid and famed newspaper columnist, has said ... "a family is many generations closely woven; that though the generations may die, they endure as part of the fabric of the family... . We carry the dead generations within us and pass them on to the future aboard our children. This keeps the people of the past alive long after we have carried them to the churchyard."

In spite of the disagreements on the value of genealogical findings in any search for identity, I believe that I should at least consider the potential influence of ancestor's lives on my own identity. After all, I can always discard any knowledge I gain from my discoveries. Apparently, I am not the only interested party who puts some stock in the events and historical milieu his ancestors experienced. Several television programs have emphasized the significance of our ancestors.

I am an ardent fan of a television series called *Finding Your Roots*, produced by the Corporation for Public Broadcasting. The show is hosted by Henry Louis Gates, Jr., a Harvard professor. Begun in 2012, the program has been updated and still runs regularly on select PBS television channels. It is now in its fifth season. Gates is especially effective when he draws out from his guests their emotions at learning the identities and the notable stories of their newly-discovered ancestors. Many of the guests seem emotionally moved, and it is a rare guest who does not allude to his/her need to assimilate the new information. One imagines what these guests are doing is trying to find ways to change their respective beliefs about whom they are and what they stand for. In short, I believe that they are rearranging, however slightly, their identity, their sense of self.

So it is with me. I feel a need to rethink my identity, partly based on my personal achievements over the years, but also to no small degree, on the discoveries I have made about both my paternal and maternal ancestors.

On both my father's side of the family and especially on my mother's paternal side, I find I come from a long line of religious people—enthusiastic practitioners of their respective faiths. Some of these religiously-oriented "goody-two-shoes" in my ancient family were Catholic and Anglican saints. To repeat, there were Saints Chlotilde, Begga, Itta, Bertha, Margaret of Scotland, and Arnulf, the Bishop of Metz, and his wife, Dode. In the Protestant and Orthodox churches, another person revered as a saint is the Reverend Dr. Rowland Taylor.

My father's roots were simpler. He came from a line of hard-working shepherds, laborers and farmers. Family tradition has said that his roots are found in Poland. But, I recently discovered that they were relative newcomers to that land. Before my father's death, I had his Y-DNA tested. Rather than belonging to the typical Polish Y-DNA group known as *Haplogroup R*, he tested as *N1C1*, a type quite unknown in Poland, but common in Finland, Estonia, Latvia, Siberia, and Lithuania. The family's move to Poland must have occurred sometime before 1800, since both my father's paternal Chylinski ancestors and his maternal Sobocinski forebears lived in Poland from the eighteenth century onward.

So my father's male antecedents whether they realized it or not were not long-time Poles. Genetically at least, they did not quite fit in their adopted nation. Further, when my father's father came to the United States about 1910, he did not quite fit in America either. As an eastern European and Catholic immigrant in a largely Protestant country--and a rather biased, anti-Catholic, anti-immigrant one at that--he may have experienced a sense of displacement, carrying with him feelings of estrangement, while living the life of an outsider. I never knew my father's father, and I deem this a great loss. He died of colon-rectal cancer in 1940, years before I was born. I have never even seen a photograph of him. A tragic house fire in my paternal grandmother's house occurred in the early 1950s on Rathbun Avenue in the heart of *Krakowa*. All of the known family photographs went up in smoke in that blaze. Fortunately, my grandmother and two uncles who were living in that house all survived. The house itself and all its contents were completely destroyed.

There we have it—two obvious patterns that appear in my ancient and more modern family. The first pattern is that the family often held membership in a sometimes anti-establishment, religious group. Forebears such as Chlotilde, Itta, Begga, Bertha, Arnulf of Metz, Rowland Taylor, and Margaret of Scotland struggled to "keep the faith" in a strange and wild era--the Middle Ages. These ancestors lived among barely-civilized tribes including pagan Vikings,

Ostrogoths, Visigoths, as well as scores of rebellious religious heretics.

The second pattern in my ancient family is that of membership in a political out-group, often forcing them to fight for acceptance in a foreign or strange environment. For the Reverend Dr. Rowland Taylor, it was a case of struggling to maintain his theological views in his own homeland. For much of his adult life, the battle between the Catholicism of Rome and the Protestant faith of England and northern Europe created an unsafe environment for him, depending on the faith practices of the monarch on the English throne.

In a way, many of these well-known and previously hidden ancestors are heroes to me. They survived difficult and dangerous times while making a name for themselves in world history. In childhood, my heroes were largely baseball players and even my parents. Now some of my heroes are historical characters. My pattern of hero worship has certainly changed. And I sometimes wonder if someday, I will be a hero to some as-yet-unborn descendant. Might I already be a hero to someone unknown to me?

But how do I fit into the patterns of my long-dead ancestors? I am not sure I have a bullet-proof explanation. Perhaps these patterns are simply human phenomena that we all can identify with to some degree. I do not know.

Still, I have seen traces of these patterns repeated in my own life. One, the struggle to fit in, to feel like I belonged, has been a common theme in my life. The second theme, trying to maintain my sense of self and my own beliefs in a world that might not approve of who I am, is related to that first issue. I have asked myself many times, "What is the approval of others worth to me? Would there be psychological or emotional costs involved in getting the approval of others? Would I be willing to pay these costs to be accepted socially?" While I can imagine that these themes are common in many human beings, I know that my own struggles with these issues continue today.

On the maternal side of my family, I was quite sure based on a preconceived notion of the Irish sound of his last name that my grandfather's roots were in Ireland. Yet, rather than finding Grandpa Powers' ancestors in Ireland, I discovered that his ancestors came from England, France, Belgium, Germany, the Low Countries, Spain, and Scandinavia—everywhere except Ireland. The closest I came to finding an Irish connection was in my multiple times great-grandfather, John Lackland. Known as "Bad King John," Lackland was appointed ruler of Ireland by his father, Henry II, in 1185. His stay in Ireland was anything but successful. The people of Ireland learned to despise John rather quickly, and he left after only eight months on that island. It is unlikely he ever returned, given his troubles elsewhere in his kingdom. John also lost much of his family's lands in France and some in England later in his reign.

Many of William Powers' ancestors died when quite young—no shock there as life expectancy was only in the late 20s or 30s for early medieval residents. Yet, I was surprised to learn how many young people died in childbirth—both mothers and their children. Some who survived childbirth would die just days or months later, a result of poor post-natal care, infections, or rapidly debilitating diseases.

This has been quite the genealogical journey. It was like a trip back in time for me. Although I studied history in school, the Middle Ages was not my forte. I admit that to write this book, I had to learn a lot about European and Middle Eastern history during the period 500 A.D. to the mid-sixteenth century. Records were scarce, and those that did exist were often biased, or incomplete. Fortunately, many of William Powers' ancestors were well-known enough or well-respected enough that I could at least find some reliable information about them.

A general summary of Bill Powers' female ancestors, i.e. his great-grandmothers, seems appropriate here. Looking for common threads among these women, one obvious connection is that all of them I have reported here had been nobles and aristocrats. That in itself is not so amazing. What is surprising is that at a time when women were considered like children—second class beings who had best be seen rather than heard—so many of William Powers' female ancestors were outspoken, sometimes wealthy, and often downright powerful in their own right.

Certainly the twenty-six women described in my book, *Family Secrets*, were not people to be ignored or dismissed lightly. Beginning with St. Chlotilde in the fifth century down through Sancha of Provence (and her rival for her husband's affections, Joan de Valletorte), these were strong women—women who were ahead of their time. Most were role models that 20th century practitioners of female liberation could have been proud to emulate.

Further, nearly all of the women that I described in *Family Secrets* were noblewomen who helped to rule their own or their spouse's kingdoms or duchies in a period even before there were nation-states. France was not France, but was the Kingdom of Burgundy or Neustria or Austrasia. England was not a nation, but was a series of small kingdoms such as Mercia, Kent, Wessex, and Northumbria. And finally, Spain was not yet Spain, but was a group of mini-kingdoms called Navarre, Castile, Aragon, and Leon. Many of my great-grandparents resided in these pre-nation geographic areas.

Still another thread these women held in common was that so many of them were personally in touch with the movers and shakers of medieval history. Certainly, their husbands had in many cases, a great impact on European history. But additionally, some of these women personally knew popes like Gregory the Great, Innocent III, and Honorius III. They corresponded with the clergy in Rome either by letter or by personal visits to the Vatican.

Most of them shared the fact that they and/or their husbands had made substantial donations to the Church—gifts of land, the building of abbeys, many of which still exist today, and donations of precious jewels and other artifacts. It is no wonder that many of William Powers' female ancestors received so much respect from the Catholic clergy.

The women described in *Family Secrets* not only witnessed medieval history, they were the flesh-and-blood characters who populate history books, and they helped to fill the annals of world and European history. They watched empires rise and fall, and kings and queens come and go. Some welcomed a spouse home from the Crusades, and in the case of Eleanor of Aquitaine, one of them actually participated in those Middle Eastern battles for Christianity. Still others struggled in other ways for personal power, and/or for their personal faith.

They traveled by horseback or in wagons without shock absorbers for long distances to far-flung places on roads that were barely passable. They sailed the ocean blue fraught with dangers like pirates. Some watched Viking invaders sack monasteries and churches. They saw children and wives taken away as spoils of war, and some watched their babies die early and painful deaths. And they prayed that they and their families would live yet another day, when death through disease, war, or violence waited just over the next horizon.

They attended Mass, whether to impress their neighbors, or to keep gossip about their faithlessness to a minimum, or like St. Chlotilde, St. Begga, St. Itta, St. Bertha, and St. Margaret of Scotland, because they were truly pious women, people who felt close to God, and who did not care who knew.

These female ancestors often found themselves as political pawns of their husbands or their fathers, commodities whose fate lay within the hands of those who wanted to further their own ends. In fairness though, some of these ancestral women were not all that gentle or kind themselves. A few, like Queen Brunhilda, held violent grudges. Some slept around with or without their husband's knowledge. One, Isabelle of Angouleme, stole a husband from her daughter. And like several of the husbands, they sought annulments or outright divorces or repudiations just so they could remarry a "better" brand of spouse.

A few fought ruthlessly alongside their personal troops, against their own husbands as they grasped for land, power, and even to impress potential suitors. Those same husbands may themselves have been sleeping around. John Lackland, for example is purported to have had over 20 illegitimate children. And between affairs, some of these husbands were busy fighting wars they themselves started or they were busy murdering their spouse or hiring others to commit murder against their rivals, like Fulk V and perhaps King John, who was accused of killing his nephew, Arthur.

Many of the women described in *Family Secrets* worked behind the scenes using indirect power to influence their native or adopted homelands. Urraca, Anna Yaroslavna, and Hildegarde of Metz come to mind here. Still others were more active and direct in their use of power, e.g. Melisende, the Queen of Jerusalem, Matilda, the Queen of Germany and Empress of the Holy Roman Empire, and Emma, the wife of two kings, Aethelred and Cnut.

And then, there was Matilda de Cornwall Walcott. Matilda was on the very end of a line of powerful, wealthy, and influential female ancestors who had lived hundreds of years earlier in France, Scandinavia, Germany, Belgium, and elsewhere. Heaven knows she must have done her best to maintain an air of royal dignity as her sister ancestors had done. She was still called *Lady*, and her husband was still called *Sir Knight*, but they were now near the bottom of the feudal pecking order.

Gone were most of Matilda's ancestors' lands, castles, and wealth.

Still, she did have her own manor house and probably had servants. She could at least maintain her bragging rights about her forebears. And she could claim (if only she had known) to have great grandmothered (is there such a word?) the first of her family to journey to the New World. That great-grandson would go on to become a legislator and an Assistant to the Governor of the freshly-minted colony of Connecticut during the seventeenth century in America. His name was John Mason (1600-1672).

To say the least, my search was a fascinating trip across the centuries, starting just four hundred and seventy-five years after the birth of Christ. Roman soldiers may still have inhabited Britain and Gaul during the birth of St. Chlotilde. The journey in which I sought ancient ancestors ended with Matilda de Cornwall in the late Middle Ages at the edge of early modern times. Truthfully, the discovery of so many unexpected ancestors has been thrilling, and a treat I would not want to have missed.

Sitting in a dusty courthouse or at an out-of-town library trying to find evidence about my "Papaw's" and "Mamaw's" ancestors has been difficult work, but simultaneously exhilarating. Each research day felt like I was opening an unexpected gift at Christmas or receiving an unpredicted award. There always seemed to be another reward just around the corner. There were so many unique insights and astonishing moments to be had. The research portion of the journey, while long—35 years to be exact—and arduous, now seems worth every moment. You will have to pardon me if I take a silent moment to congratulate myself for publishing the work. And if it is not well-done, then at least the results are workmanlike!

While writing that book about the women in Grandpa's life, I not only wanted to share my research results with my living relatives, I found myself wanting to build some sort of time machine, so I could meet an ancestor or two in the flesh. But who would I want to meet? And who would I want to avoid meeting? Although the answer to each of these questions is purely dream work, there is an additional problem here. I would be judging these ancestors by my 21st century values and by my prior personal experiences. Historians have a word for this dilemma—*zeitgeist*.

We are a product of our own time in history. And we are shaped by our personal and cultural environment. Still, given these limitations, I find myself wanting to sit down with St. Bertha, the

Saxon queen, and a woman who personally wrote to, and even met St. Augustine. I would also like to meet St. Margaret of Scotland. Historians have described her work with the poor of her kingdom as an inspirational model. Rather than serving the poor "cleanly"--their word, not mine, she served others by getting her hands "dirty." These historians have noted that "clean service" involves giving money or possessions, while "dirty service" includes performing acts such as washing the feet of the poor as did Margaret and her husband, Malcolm. Now I have to ask myself, what it is about these two women that I find so attractive? And I don't yet know the answer.

And for the opposite end of the spectrum, who would I not want to meet? There are numerous candidates for that honor. There is Brunhilda, the Queen of Austrasia and Burgundy. She had a decades-long violent and vindictive dispute with her rival, Fredegunde during much of the sixth century. Her life ended badly—she was physically torn apart by four wild horses after spending days being tortured by one of Fredegunde's associates. Fredegunde fared better, dying of natural causes years before Brunhilda.

Then, there was Isabelle of Angouleme and her husband, John Lackland. Neither would be on my list of favorites. John was arguably the absolute worst monarch in the history of England. Instead of ruling England effectively, he spent much of his time losing a substantial part of his kingdom, while producing many children by many different relationships. In his favor, he at least provided for the upkeep of his two dozen or so offspring.

As for Isabelle, she corresponded with Pope Honorius II at least five times and dozens of times with her son, King Henry III, offering him advice and encouragement. But she also "stole" her daughter's fiancé out from under her. Ironically perhaps, the man she took from her daughter was the son of her own former fiancé, Hugh de Lusignan. Earlier, the elder Hugh had been banished from England and from Isabelle by her eventual husband, King John. John and Isabelle seem to have deserved each other! Such irony is not lost on historians.

But, alas! There is no time machine, so I will not likely meet any of these forebears, whether I am drawn to them or not. It is a pity that I cannot share these stories with my mother, with her father, the late Bill Powers, or with Bill's son, the late James Floyd Powers. James died quite suddenly and unexpectedly in 2015. He was always interested in knowing about his ancestors, and for decades he encouraged me to write a book about our family. I did him one better and wrote two books, one about his maternal ancestors and the other about his paternal forebears.

Further, I am sorry that Uncle James did not live long enough to not only hear about his relatives, but to see their lives recreated in print. Still, there is some consolation for me in that I can now leave something behind for readers who might be interested in medieval history in general, or in the tales of William Henry Powers' and Mary Underwood Powers' forebears.

But has any of this information about my ancestors altered my sense of self? I am afraid not. For one reason, I carry very little of the DNA of these ancestors. I attribute more of who I am to my parents' and grandparents' genetic contributions than I do to long dead ancestors. Further, it appears that all of us are much more closely related to one another than previously thought. It seems foolhardy to boast about ancient forebears when recent research indicates we are all cousins! But I'll say more about these relationships later.

DNA test results, ethnicity estimates, and my search for identity

The paper trail that helped me to discover my ancestors is not the end of the story in my search for identity. In fact, that trail may be only the beginning of the journey.

Some months ago, I conducted a DNA test on myself, thanks to an offer from the web site, www.MyHeritage.com. After paying what seemed like a reasonable price ($69.00) for a self-administered DNA testing kit, I waited for a week or so for the kit to arrive in the mail. Following the directions on the test kit carefully, I swabbed the inner portion of my cheeks with what looked like an elongated Q-tip. I then inserted the fancy Q-tip into a test tube-like apparatus, and sealed it. That same day, I rushed to my local post office to send my DNA material to the company's laboratory for analysis.

My wait for the results seemed like an eternity. But, several weeks later, I received an e-mail from *MyHeritage*, showing me in full color the ancient roots of my family. To say I was surprised would be an understatement. The results were arranged in a vertical column on the left side of each page of the multi-page report, with an outline map of my family's geographic location(s) shown on the right. The data on the left were listed in descending order from highest ethnic proportions to lowest, and began with the percentages of my DNA that could be traced to Northern and Western Europe.

I felt no shock waves when I read that I carried 27.5% Scandinavian DNA. After all, the paper trail indicated that I was a direct descendant of Rollo "the Viking" and Harald I, King of Denmark. Under the heading, "British and Irish", the data showed that 26% of my DNA had its origin in those areas. Again, I felt no surprise since the paper trail supported my descent from Queen Emma and King Alfred "the Great" of England, as well as Eleanor of Aquitaine and both of her husbands, Louis VII and Henry II.

Nor was I aghast when I read that I carried 5% Iberian DNA. Some of my ancestors from that part of the world included Petronilla Ramirez, Sancha of Castile, and Alfonso II. The real surprises included the following data:

Ashkenazi Jewish	0.8%
West Asian	1.4%
East African Maasai	2.7%

Wow! Who would have guessed at such an admixture? Certainly not my parents had they been alive at the time of these discoveries. Once my initial shock had subsided, and I was able to think more clearly and less emotionally, I have slowly begun to "own" my newly-found ethnicities.

But wait! After integrating these ethnicity findings into my sense of self, I still felt curious. I took another DNA test using the same cheek-swabbing technique. This time the testing company that I used was FamilyTreeDNA, whose laboratory in Houston, Texas has a reputation for accuracy. For better or for worse FamilyTreeDNA's reported results were vastly different than those of MyHeritage.com. The Texas-based laboratory found that my DNA was 99% European! It listed no subgroups such as Iberians, or Scandinavians, and certainly not Africans or Asians!

Oh my! What's a person to do with such contrasting results? Of course, I sent for another DNA test, this time from the venerable genealogical site, www.ancestry.com. It will be fascinating to compare the findings of these three companies. I have not yet decided what I will do if *ancestry's* laboratory discovers yet another ethnic background for me. I will soon exhaust my testing funds.

These discrepancies are seemingly common. In a "study", admittedly an unscientific one conducted by the television program *Inside Edition*, its researchers administered DNA tests to three sets of identical triplets, and on a set of indistinguishable quadruplets. One set of triplets was given the 23andmeDNA test, the second set was given the FamilyTreeDNA genetic test, while the third set of triplets was administered the AncestryDNA test. Results for each member of each set of triplets and quadruplets ought to have produced identical results.

Indeed, with the first set of triplets, all of the sisters were 99% European. Yet, 23andMe found that one sister was only 11% French and German, while the second triplet was 22.3% French and German. The final triplet was deemed 18% ethnic French and German.

For the second set of triplets, all three had their roots in Great Britain, but differed in the percentages of DNA from the British Isles. One sister had 59% of such DNA, while her sisters had 66% and 70 percent, respectively. The tests also showed that one sister had six percent Scandinavian roots, while her sisters showed none. The final set of triplets was nearly identical in their ethnic roots. These latter triplets had tested with the AncestryDNA laboratory. As for the quadruplets, their DNA, which was analyzed by 23andMe, produced nearly identical results.
https://www.insideedition.com/investigative/21784-how-reliable-are-home-dna-ancestry-tests-investigation-uses-triplets   Retrieved 8/20/2018.

The point here is that DNA testing for ethnicity is sketchy at best. Results need to be taken with a grain of salt, and results will likely differ from testing company to testing company. While all testing laboratories have strengths and some weaknesses, there had been rumors circulating that the first company I used to test my DNA, MyHeritage.com, was a bit sloppy in reporting their results to their customers. In fairness to MyHeritage, it should be said that beginning in early 2017, the company vastly improved the quality of their analyses. In fact, they now include 42 ethnic regions of the world in their ethnic estimates. The company's accuracy for ethnic make-up of a tested individual must now be given high marks. https://dna-explained.com/2017/05/30/myheritage-ethnicity-results   Retrieved 8/20/2018.

Yet, the results of my first ethnicity test with MyHeritage.com remind me of some not-so-pleasant events from my childhood in Cleveland. I recall that my so-called friends, Buddy, Brian, and Richard, sometimes taunted me when they felt like doing so. And "when they felt like it", usually meant when we were on the outs, that is when they were mad at me or simply wanted to feel better about themselves by attempting to make me feel worse about myself.

The nickname they chose for me that was designed to get a negative response from me was "Chinaman." I have to admit, my skin was dark and my heavier than typical eyelids did give me the appearance of a non-white person. What a revelation it was to discover that with MyHeritage's ethnicity-finder DNA test results it is possible that these boys were right on the money with their analysis of my ethnicity. Their choice of that particular racial slur may have been based on something they saw or sensed in me. Could it have been an unconscious observation that led them to that nickname? Is a DNA test result of 1.4% West Asian enough to give me an Asian look? Maybe.

But now in the 21st century, rather than hearing that racial slur with some pain—it was intended to be derogatory--I felt pride that I carried a small amount of Asian blood. How wonderful!!! As for my African roots, I felt a genuine swelling of pride in my breast. One of my all-time favorite movies was a Michael Douglas' film, *The Ghost and the Darkness*. Featured heavily in this film were Maasai warriors, a tribe renowned for seeking out man-eating lions with nothing more than a spear. Maybe these were my people! Again, Wow! Wow! Wow!

All this information on my Asian and Massai ancestors may be fascinating to some, but personally I am faced with a new dilemma. And the dilemma is a familiar one to me. I have returned to a question that had been haunting me since childhood—WHO AM I? I now had to fit this new information into my existing answer to that question. Truthfully, I have not yet come to any firm, revised decision about the totality of my ethnic identity. Getting contrasting results from the two DNA laboratories has led to additional confusion for me.

I am not alone in discovering African roots. The fact is that looking far enough into the distant past all of us are either Africans or we are descended from Africans. Evidence is clear that human life almost certainly began in East Africa, probably near the border of Kenya and Tanzania. Ironically, this area of the continent is also home to the Maasai people.

Archeological evidence has shown that genetically-human beings first appeared in sub-Saharan Africa about 140,000 years ago. Small groups of these humans began migrating out of Africa in waves beginning about 100,000 years ago. So like it nor not, we are each just varying shades of black. In short, there is only one race, and that is

African. It seems rather certain based on recent research, that I am not alone in having African roots. To repeat, there is only one race--African! Knowing that all of us are either Africans or are descended from Africans certainly takes a bit of the shine from my pride over my supposed African Maasai roots! http://adversity.net/FRAMES/Editorials54_Paler_Shade_of_Black. Retrieved 10/28/2017.

Yet, in spite of the discrepancies of ethnicity reports made by the various DNA testing companies, such testing can still be useful in tracing family. Several DNA testing laboratories make periodic announcements to their customers when potential "relatives" appear to share long strands of DNA. Shared strands of DNA typically mean shared relationships.

Eight billion cousins and my search for identity

Genetic evidence also appears to indicate that all of us are at least fiftieth cousins, in some cases, several times removed. The reason this is true has to do with a phenomenon called *pedigree collapse*. The collapse in ancestor numbers works like this: Each of us has two biological parents, four grandparents, eight great-grandparents, and so forth. Tracing back ten generations, each of us would have 1024 direct ancestors (that is, grandparents). Could this possibly be true? Probably not! The current best guess is that about eighty percent of all marriages in history were between second cousins. This fact alone means that fewer separate ancestors are available.

And going back thirty generations, each person's direct ancestors would number more than the world's entire population at the time! An impossibility surely, but the reality is that many of our ancestors married at least one of their cousins, intentionally or otherwise. Such intermarriage shrinks the family tree, as husband and wife then share branches on the family tree of the other.

In fact, medieval nobles (including some of my distant ancestors) often deliberately sought to marry their cousins thereby keeping wealth and property in the family. Still, given the small population centuries ago, and the fact that people lived in small communities and seldom left their own village, there simply were not very many available marriage partners except if individuals married cousins.

Likely the most acceptable theory of ancestor growth and ancestral duplication is the *diamond theory*. According to the diamond theory, the list of ancestors, when arranged graphically, resembles a pyramid. You and I are at the top of each of our own pyramids, while each of our parents are immediately below us, and our four respective grandparents, are listed below them, with each of our eight great-grandparents just below them on the chart.

The diamond theory of ancestor growth and duplication of grandparents also states that the pyramid of our grandparents begins to narrow following the tenth generation back in time. Why? Because there are fewer and fewer available ancestors, and therefore we begin to accumulate cousins—that is, we begin share ancestors.

It is estimated that by the 14th generation back, we theoretically have eight thousand, one hundred and ninety-two grandparents. By the sixteenth generation, we theoretically have thirty-two thousand, seven hundred and sixty-eight grandparents.

Yet, these numbers are only theoretical, since we also share many of our grandparents with ourselves. In other words, we have redundant ancestors. For example, William Henry Powers (my maternal grandfather) is a grandson of Charlemagne twice along his ancestral line, and he is a grandson of Louis VI twice in his line. This is mind-boggling for me to try to comprehend, but it is nevertheless true on some level for me, for William Powers, and for each of us! What this mathematical phenomenon also does for us is that it makes it more and more likely that we have thousands and thousands of cousins that we share—making most, if not all of us, probable cousins as well. http://olivetreegenealogy.com/misc/ancestors/shtml Retrieved 4/6/2016.

Given the array of sizes, shapes and colors of human beings alive today, some may find the theory that we-are-all-cousins unbelievable. I can hear them ask "How could we have cousins who look so different than we do?" Yet, no matter what the color, ethnicity, or nationality of these cousins, most of us we are at least 50th cousins, and are possibly even closer than that!

If the all-of-us-are-cousins theory is mathematically correct, then my ancestors, famous or not, are also your cousins. How is that for taking some of the shine off both my historical and genetic discoveries about my identity?

Some final thoughts on identity

"My name is Chylinski, Steve   Date: October 28 Height in inches: = 43.5 Weight = 42.75 Gain in Weight = minus .75"

This information is taken from the Harvard Elementary School document, *"My Weight Record"*

I found the above document in some of my mother's things following her death in 2012. While I felt somewhat honored that she saved this identification from the 1950s, I was also bewildered. Is this my core identity? Am I just a listing of my given name, height, weight, weight change, and the name of the school that I attended on October 28? Surely, I must be more than a set of statistics.

When I taught psychology to not-so-eager-to-learn college freshmen, I asked them to take out a clean sheet of paper, and write the words, "I Am…" twenty times. They were then to complete each line with some statement of their identity. Their answers, not surprisingly, included their vital information such as:

> I am a female
> I am a Methodist
> I am 5'3" tall
> I am an immigrant

and so forth. These students seldom did more than scratch their own surfaces.

Of course, this question of identity goes much deeper than that. And the deeper answers one gives can be ever-changing, since development goes on for a lifetime. This is true for me as well. I am not sure I can answer this intriguing question of who I am any more thoroughly now than I could at the beginning of this memoir, nor in so short a space. What a disappointment not to be able to give some succinct (but certainly glib) answer to this important question!

I certainly have changed since childhood. The process of change has been a series of small steps, each altering who I am in some minute way. While I've maintained my base identity—shy, frightened of some things and some people, bright, motivated, hard-working, and adventurous—I've also made some improvements.

Perhaps the most significant improvement has been a willingness to take risks in spite of the potential physical, emotional, and spiritual dangers involved. In short, I have "stretched" beyond my largely-inherited personality and far beyond any expectations I had for myself in childhood and adolescence.

It seems to me that such "stretching" (of what we were and what we could become) is a key to creating life experiences. In turn, those life experiences can lead to a revised and newly-identifiable "me." The way I think about myself now is a direct result of my core personality, deliberate stretching that is risk-taking, my life experiences, and other factors.

Here I suppose I could re-examine the list of the separate kinds of identity that constitute "me." These are enumerated on the second page of this final section of this memoir. The alternative kinds of identity include the relationship me, the academic me, the religious me, and so forth. Yet, to do so seems rather tedious and a bit boring. Besides, re-hashing the list of identity types is not likely to reveal my identity any more accurately than I have already.

At this point in life—my 70s—I am not sure I want to change or grow a lot more. Near the last decades of my life, I am content to reflect on what I have done—my accomplishments. I ask myself regularly: What have I really done with my life? Am I satisfied? Do I have regrets? Is there any unfinished business I want to complete? Are there things I need to say to someone, anyone? Shall I ask for forgiveness from_____? Are there places or people I would like to see in the time I have left?

Yes, this is a time for reflection. I have always liked thinking. Now that I need not worry about a career, or finding a partner, or making a living, I have the luxury of just thinking. Part of my reflection will be to continue answering the question "Who Am I?" but also to ask myself "Is the world any better off that I existed?"

As for my genealogical discoveries, I find them interesting, fun, and even exciting to have these revealed to me, but they are not me. And my ancestors may have had some little influence on the person I have become, but their contributions to my identity are slight. That goes for my DNA test results as well. I find my ethnic diversity fascinating, but not all that significant to my identity.

To repeat, many variables have made me who I am today—my life experiences, my core personality, DNA test results, and other factors. On the one hand, I feel somewhat important because of my accomplishments. On the other hand, many thousands of my cousins have done as much or more. Suffice it to say, I have made some contributions to my family and to others I have come into contact with during my lifetime.

For now, I will put my initial question—Who Am I?—on a shelf possibly to be looked at later. In the meantime, I will sit quietly in my rocking chair, grandchildren playing nearby, and reflect on what it all means. It has been a great ride! As for my role as tale-teller, I am still not positive why I chose to become the family story-teller, but I am thrilled that someone in the family took up that task. After all, the stories I've recounted are now recorded in writing. They will be available to anyone who finds such tales valuable for decades or possibly for centuries to come.

Over the past weekend, I attended the Underwood family reunion in Kentucky. The Underwood clan was my maternal grandmother's people. I spoke with a handful of my cousins, some of whom I met for the first time. As I listened to them tell me bits of their own family stories, I realized what a joy it is to have a family, and to stay connected with them.

My hope for each of these reunion party-goers is that they can find some way to keep their own family tales alive through telling and re-telling them. Their reminiscences seem so precious to me. Stories are the way that families live on. As the torch is passed from one generation to the next, family stories can go on and on so that our ancestors will be known long after they have been carried to the graveyard.

Not only are we charged with discovering our own identities, we can hunt for the identities of our forebears as well giving them voice though they are long gone. Happy hunting!

References

Ball, E. (2007). *The genetic strand: Exploring a family history through DNA.* New York: Simon & Schuster.

Bouchard, T.J., Lykken, D.T., McGue, M., Segal, N.L., & Tellegen, A. (1990) Sources of human psychological differences: The Minnesota study of twins reared apart. *Science, Vol. 250,* No. 4978, pp. 223-228.

Colletta, J.P. 2002). *They came in ships: A guide to finding your immigrant ancestor's arrival record.* Nashville, TN: Turner Publishing.

Costello, V. (2011). *The complete idiot's guide to writing a memoir.* New York: Penguin Books.

Crackell, T.J. (2007). *The papers of George Washington, digital edition.* Charlottesville, VA: University of Virginia Press.

Erikson, E.H. (1968). *Identity: Youth and Crisis.* New York: Norton.

Erikson, E. (Fall 1970). "Identity Crisis" in Autobiographic Perspective. *Daedalus 99.* The Making of Modern Science: Biographical Studies, pp. 730-759.

Faris, D. (2006). *Plantagenet ancestry of seventeenth-century colonists.* Baltimore: Genealogical Publishing.

Felman, A. (2018). Neuroses and neuroticism: What's the difference? https//www.medicalnewstoday.com/articles/246608/php Retrieved 1/29/2018.

Foxe, J. (1563). *Actes and monuments of these latter and perilous days, touching matters of the church.* London, Day Publishers.

Goleman, D. (1986). Personality study finds that traits are mostly inherited. http://www.nytimes.com/1986/12/02/science/major-personality-study-finds-that-traits-are-mostly-inherited.html Retrieved 1/31/2018.

Habermas, T., & de Silveira, C. (2008). The development of global coherence in life narrative across adolescence: Temporal, causal, and thematic aspects. *Developmental Psychology, 44,* pp. 707-721.

Haley, A. (1976). *Roots: The saga of an American family.* New York: Doubleday.

Hedley, R. K. (2003). *Married well and often: Marriages of the Northern Neck of Virginia, 1649-1800.* Baltimore: Genealogical Publishing.

https://en.wikipedia.org/wiki/Identity_formation. Retrieved 3/23/2018.

https://www.psychologytoday.com/blog/fulfillment-any-age/201203/are-you-having-identity-crisis Retrieved 12/20/2017.

http://www.innovateus.net/innopedia/when-can-person-have-identity-crisis Retrieved 12/20/2017.

Kopp, S. (1972). *If you meet the Buddha on the road, kill him*! Science and Behavior Books: Palo Alto, CA.

Kopp, S. (1991). *All God's children are lost, but only a few can play the piano.* Prentice Hall: New York

Lahey, B.B. (2009). Public health significance of neuroticism. *American Psychologist, (4),* pp. 241-256.

Lefer, D. (2013). *The founding conservatives: How a group of unsung heroes saved the American Revolution.* New York: The Penguin Group.

Lopez, de Victoria, S. (2014). Beware of She-Wolves. *Psych Central.* https://psychcentral.com/blog/archives/2014/02/11/beware-of-she-wolves/ Retrieved 10-19-2015.

Marcia, J.E. (1966). "Development and validation of ego identity status". *Journal of Personality and Social Psychology, 3.* pp. 551-559.

McAdams, D. P. (2001). The psychology of life stories. *Review of General Psychology, 5* (2), pp. 100-122.

McAdams, D. P. (2013). *The redemptive self: Stories Americans live by.* New York: Oxford University Press.

McAdams, D.P. (2018). www.nobaproject.com Retrieved 1/22/2018.

McCrae, R.R., & Costa, P.T. (1992). An introduction to the five factor model and its applications. *Journal of Personality and Social Psychology, 60* (2). pp. 175-215.

McLean, K.C., & Fournier, M. (2008). The content and processes of autobiographical reasoning in narrative identity. *Journal of Research in Personality, 42,* pp. 527-545.

Palmer, P.J. (2008). The heart of a teacher: Identity and integrity in teaching. (http://www.mcli.dist.maricopa.edu/events/afc99/articles/heartof.pdf) Retrieved 12/20/2017.

Pasupathi, M. (2001). The social construction of the personal past and its implications for adult development. *Psychological Bulletin, 127,* pp. 651-672.

Powers, A.H. (1884). *The Powers family: A genealogical and historical record of Walter Power and some of his descendants to the ninth generation.* Chicago: Fergus Publishing.

Powers-Chylinski, S. (2015). *Saints, sinners, scoundrels, and some ordinary people: The Virginia, Kentucky, and European ancestors of Mary Underwood Powers.* Create Space Publishing: North Charleston, SC.

Powers-Chylinski, S. (2016). *Family secrets: Discovering medieval queens.* Create Space Publishing: North Charleston, SC.

Schaap. R. (2013). *Drinking with men: A memoir.* New York: Riverhead Books.

Scherman, K. (1987). *The birth of France: Warriors, bishops, and long-haired kings.* New York: Random House.

Smolenyak, M.S., & Turner, A. (2004). *Trace your roots with DNA: Using genetic tests to explore your family tree.* Stuggart: Holtzbrinck Publishers.

Temes, R. (2013). *How to write a memoir in 30 days.* New York: Reader's Digest.

Waterman, A.S. (2001). "Finding someone to be: Studies on the role of intrinsic motivation in identity formation." *Identity: International Journal of Theory and Research.*

Wells, S. (2002). *The journey of man: A genetic odyssey.* Princeton, NJ: Princeton University Press.

Appendix 1: The Path from William Henry Powers to Clovis

Name	Relationship to William Powers
William Henry Powers	
George W. Powers	Father
Ira Powers	Grandfather
(Reverend) George W. Powers	Great-grandfather
Elizabeth Cooley Powers	2 X Great-grandmother
Benjamin Cooley II	3 X Great-grandfather
Benjamin Cooley I	4 X Great-grandfather
Elizabeth Walcott Cooley	5 X Great-grandmother
Simon Walcott	6 X Great-grandfather
Henry Walcott	7 X Great-grandfather
John Walcott II	8 X Great-grandfather
John Walcott I	9 X Great-grandfather
Thomas Walcott	10 X Great-grandfather
William Walcott II	11 X Great-grandfather
William Walcott I	12 X Great-grandfather
Roger Walcott	13 X Great-grandfather
Matilda Walcott Cornwall	14 X Great-grandmother
Richard de Cornwall	15 X Great-grandfather

Geoffrey de Cornwall	16 X Great-grandfather
Richard de Cornwall	17 X Great-grandfather
Geoffrey de Cornwall	18 X Great-grandfather
Richard Plantagenet	19 X Great-grandfather
Richard Plantagenet	20 X Great-grandfather
John Lackland, King of England	21 X Great-grandfather
Henry II, King of England	22 X Great-grandfather
Geoffrey V "le Bon," Count of Anjou	23 X Great-grandfather
Foulques/Fulk V, Count of Anjou	24 X Great-grandfather
Foulques/Fulk IV, Count of Anjou	25 X Great-grandfather
Ermengarde, Countess of Anjou	26 X Great-grandmother
Fulk III, "the Black"	27 X Great-grandfather
Adelaide, Countess of Anjou	28 X Great-grandmother
Robert, Count of Vermandois	29 X Great-grandfather
Hildebrante, Princess of France	30 X Great-grandmother
Beatrice, Queen of France	31 X Great-grandmother
Herbert I, Count of Senlis	32 X Great-grandfather
Pepin II de St. Quentin	33 X Great-grandfather
Bernard, King of Italy	34 X Great-grandfather
Pepin I, King of Italy	35 X Great-grandfather
Charlemagne	36 X Great-grandfather
Pepin II "the Short"	37 X Great-grandfather

Charles Martel "the Hammer"	38 X Great-grandfather
Pepin II "the Fat"	39 X Great-grandfather
St. Begga	40 X Great-grandmother
Pepin I, Duke of Austrasia	41 X Great-grandfather
Theudebert II, King of Austrasia	42 X Great-grandfather
Childebert II, King of Austrasia	43 X Great-grandfather
Sigebert I, King of Austrasia	44 X Great-grandfather
Clotar/Clothar I, 'the Old"	45 X Great-grandfather
Clovis I, Salic King of All Franks	46 X Great-grandfather

Appendix 2: Mary Underwood Powers' Ancestors in America

1. William Underwood (1606-1637)
2. William Underwood (1630-1662)
3. Nathan Underwood (1708-1802)
4. George Underwood (1740-1794)
5. Jehu Underwood (1770-1828)
6. Willis Underwood (1803/1807-1911)
7. Eli Underwood (1849/1854-1942)
8. Nathan Underwood (1879-1948)
9. Mary Jane Underwood Powers (1902-1976)

Appendix 3: Some Male Ancestors Allied with the Powers Family

1. Clodio/Clodion "le Chevalu" (392/395-445/448)
2. Sigimerus I, Bishop of Auvergne (419-457)
3. St. Arnoulf de Metz (582-640)
4. Charibert II (608-631)
5. St. Warinus (c. 635-677)
6. St. Leutwin/Leudwinus, Archbishop of Treves and Laon (660-722)
7. Eyestein Throndsson, King of Hedmark (Norway) (668-710)
8. Rollo (Hrolf) Rognavaldsson (846-932)
9. Alfred "the Great" (848-901)
10. Robert I, King of France (870-923)
11. Edward I "the Elder" (871-924)
12. Garcia II King of Navarre (955-10__)
13. Aethelbert, King of England (966-1040)
14. Fulk/Foulke "the Black" (970-1040)
15. Robert II "the Pious" (972-1031)
16. Sancho III Garces King of Aragon (980-1035)
17. Henri I, King of France (1008-1068)
18. Ramiro I King of Aragon (1035-1096)
19. Sancho V Ramirez King of Aragon (1042-1096/1097)
20. Phllip I (1052-1108)
21. Henry I "Beauclerc" (1068-1135), King of England
22. Louis VI "the Fat" (1081-1137)
23. Ramiro II "the Monk" King of Aragon (1086?-1157?)
24. Ramon IV Berenguer (1113-1162)

25. Henry II Plantagenet (1133-1189)
26. Alfonso II "the Chaste" (1157-1196)
27. John Lackland (1166-1216)
28. Alfonso III (1180-1209)
29. Richard, Prince of England (1208-1272)
30. Richard de Cornwall (1360-1443)
31. John Wolcott (1400-1455)
32. Ralph Shepherd/Shepard (1603-1693)
33. Simon Wolcott (1624-1687)
34. Daniel Cooley (1651-1717)

Appendix 4: William Henry Powers' Male Ancestors Who Bore His Surname

1. Walter Power (1639-1708)
2. Thomas Power (1667-1733/1734)
3. Jeremiah Powers (1710-1791)
4. Captain Jeremiah Powers (1737-1801)
5. Reverend George W. Powers (1778-1830)
6. Ira Powers (1804-1873)
7. George Washington Powers (1839-1889)
8. William Henry Powers (1887-1966)
9. James Floyd Powers (1937-2015)

Appendix 5: A Letter Written to My Younger Self

Dear Stevie,

Oh, my God, what sadness I feel welling up in me just thinking about this assignment. Am I grieving over my lost (?) self? I feel so very protective of you. The adults in your life seem to have not protected you.

Either they discounted your fears and concerns or they yelled at you for not being tougher. Or they simply did not know about your troubles because you never told them. Did you decide on your own that you were not supposed to ask for help? Or did you sense that you were supposed to handle your own issues from an early age on? Or did you try to ask for support and did not get what you needed then just gave up asking altogether?

I am thinking back now about how you looked physically —your height and weight. I have in my possession what I think is a health card, perhaps issues by the school, Harvard Elementary in the 1950s. The card gives your height and weight as _____. You were so small then.

Now I am again feeling so protective of you, envisioning you as a five or six year old. You were a lovely child with your olive skin, dark hair and beautiful large green eyes. Why couldn't people see how **lovable** you were—a gentle little boy in need of some sort of protection? But, what did you need protection from?

Stevie, I am having difficulty separating the "new" me from the "then" me. Why is that do you imagine? Might you still exist in me somewhere, but I have not contacted you for decades? Perhaps, you are nearby and I simply do not take the time to be with you once again. Another question I cannot answer readily.

I want to walk alongside you, holding your precious little hand in mine. I want to tell you how much I love you—your innocence and sweetness. I know all you really wanted was to be loved, to be held in esteem, and to be recognized for your preciousness. Can I still do that for you in some way? Or were there particular people you wanted these things from, and now cannot get because they are gone.

Appendix 6: A History of Story-Telling

Story-telling is not new. It has been around for thousands of years, and is a part of every culture and every society. At first, story-telling was only an oral phenomenon, as someone in one generation told others in the generations that followed him/her. In the twenty-first century, stories are told both orally and in written fashion in movies, books, magazines, news media, architecture, and painting.

No one knows exactly when the first stories were begun to be told, and the answer to that implied question is lost somewhere in the mists of time. One can imagine a tribal elder sitting around a campfire in a cave in Africa or Europe with family members surrounding him or her. Out of the story-teller's mouth would come tales of great feats or cataclysmic events of long ago.

Some historians believe that the first stories were told as an excuse for failure—failure generated by flawed individuals or by some natural events such as storms or crop failures. Eventually, tribal story-tellers became respected members of the clan, regaling other members with tales of heroics. Soon, people began to look forward to story-telling days.

Stories were sometimes painted on cave walls or on rocks or on the sides of cliffs. For example, somewhere between 15,000 and 13,000 BC/BCE, a group of people in the Pyrenees Mountains of southern France drew figures of over 900 animals and at least one human being, quite possibly a hunter. The Lascaux Caves were discovered in 1940 by a group of teen-age boys.

Early stories were most often tales were recounted myths, fairy tales, ghost stories, fables, hero stories, and adventures of epic proportions. The stories were told and retold, often to people in faraway lands. It is very likely that only human beings create and then tell and retell stories, at least as far as we know.
http://www.storytellingday.net/history-of-storytelling-how-did-storytelling.html Retrieved 10/5/2016.

Evidence of slightly more recent stories can be found in the epic, Gilgamesh. Gilgamesh is the story of a Sumerian king who supposedly lived in about 3000 BC/BCE. Initially, the Gilgamesh tale was told and likely changed in the oral recounting. But samples of the tale can be seen on a clay table that was fired in about 799 BC/BCE. It was also carved on stone pillars where many people could see the story visually depicted.

And sometime between 2000-1300 BC/BCE, there was a papyrus written down by the sons of Cheops, the great pyramid builder, in which tales were retold about one of Cheops' ancestors as well as more contemporary stories. This seems to demonstrate that storytelling was used for both remembering history and for entertainment or for religious purposes. (Michael Lockett, 2007, *The Basics of Storytelling*).

Although the Greeks claim Aesop as one of their own, he was most likely a former slave who originated was born in Africa about 550 BC/BCE. His not only preserved the fables of others, but he created his own stories that have survived into modern times. His stories were not written down until 300-250 BC/BCE.

The Greeks did have their own storyteller in Homer's epics, some that were told as early as 1200 BC/BCE Not to be outdone, China and Indian both have had stories of storytelling. For instance, the Zhou dynasty (1122-256 BC/BCE) as well as epic Chinese Buddhist tales have a rich history in Asia. In India, shadow plays, using puppets to tell stories, has a history as early as 1500 BC/BCE. The shadow plays were based on epic stories about the Hindu god Rama, and were first written in Sanskrit about 1500 BC/BCE. www.mikelockett.com/downloads/HistoryofStorytelling.pdf Retrieved 12/14/2016.

Appendix 7: Fifty-two American Southernisms

1. "We're living in high cotton."
2. "You look rode hard and put up wet."
3. "He's as drunk as Cooter Brown."
4. "She's as happy as a dead pig in sunshine."
5. "I'm finer than frog hair split four ways."
6. "He thinks the sun comes up just to hear him crow."
7. "He's got enough money to burn a wet mule."
8. "That thing is all cattywampus."
9. "Well, bless your heart!"
10. "He's country as a bowl of grits."
11. "Rigor Mortis set in before he hit the water."
12. "What yer tellin' me don't amount to a 'blivit.' "
13. "If she were an inch taller she'd be round."
14. "Swingin' my legs from a dime."
15. "She's got them summer teeth."
16. "Cut da light off (or on)."
17. "Where you stay?"
18. "Ain't nobody gonna mess with me and call it apple butter!"
19. "It's hotter than a billy goat in a pepper patch."
20. "I'll knock you into the middle of next week!"
21. "That possum's on the stump."
22. "This is gooder than grits."
23. "Nervous as a long-tailed cat in a room full of rocking chairs."
24. "Dern, it's as cold as all git out this morning."
25. "Can't never could (do nothing)."
26. "I feel like I've been chewed up and spit out."
27. "Somebody throwed a clod in the churn."
28. "She could ruin a two-car funeral."
29. "Lie down with dogs and you'll get up with fleas."
30. "Can you carry me to the picture show?"
31. "It's hot as hades 'round here, IDINIT?"

32. "I believe sumpn funny's goin' on around this place."
33. "It's comin' up a cloud."
34. "It's comin' a toad-strangler."
35. "That's just a lost ball in high weeds."
36. "I feel pecked by a hundred chickens."
37. "I've got a champagne appetite and a Kool-Aid budget."
38. "He was about three sheets to the wind."
39. "Whatever cranks your tractor."
40. "Don't go borrowing trouble."
41. "It'll all come out in the wash."
42. "That dog'll hunt!"
43. "Last time I saw you, you were knee-high to a grasshopper."
44. "She's gettin' above her raisin'. "
45. "Well, butter my backside and call me a biscuit!"
46. "If I had a brain, I'd take it out and play with it."
47. "You've just traded the devil for the witch."
48. "I'm fuller than a tick on a big dog."
49. "That fits like socks on a rooster."
50. "If you're gonna have a pity party, don't invite me."
51. "All y'all."
52. "Need me some (or "get me some.")."

Also by the Author

The Royal Roots of an Indiana Coal Miner: The Ancestors of William Powers

Chylin: A Village of Their Own

The Broken Heart Experience

Denise: On the Loss of Her Son

Displaced Homemakers: The Brokenhearted in Transition

The Mysterious Tapestry: A Children's Tale

The Experience of a Broken Heart: Unpublished Doctoral Dissertation

An Unlikely Love Affair: A Biographical Sketch of Ruby Mae Powers and Steven J. Chylinski

The Nathan Underwood Family and Related Pioneers: Eleven Generations of Their Descendants in America

Pierogis and Reindeer Steaks: Discovering Ancestral Roots in the Old Country

Saints, Sinners, Scoundrels, and Some Ordinary People: The Virginia, Kentucky, and European Ancestors of Mary J. Underwood

Family Secrets: Discovering Medieval Queens

Made in the USA
Las Vegas, NV
26 February 2025

18744213R00105